How to Enjoy God's Worldwide Church

The Biblical Doctrine of the 'Universal Church'

Michael Eaton

Sovereign World

Sovereign World
PO Box 777
Tonbridge
Kent TN11 9XT
England

By the same author:
Ecclesiastes (Tyndale Commentary) – IVP
The Baptism with the Spirit – IVP
How to Live a Godly Life – Sovereign World
Walk in the Spirit – Word
Living Under Grace (Romans 6–7) – (Nelson Word)

ISBN: 1 85240 145 1

Typeset by CRB Associates, Norwich.
Printed in England by Clays Ltd, St Ives plc.

Contents

PART FOUR: Enjoying the Church

PART FIVE: The Destiny of the Church

Preface

Like a previous book of mine with a **How To** title, this book is a simple exposition of a part of Christian doctrine, this time the doctrine of the 'Universal Church'. I am restating Christian doctrine in a simple way for Christians interested in the teaching of God's Word. Although I try to write in a simple, down-to-earth manner, this is not a manual of church life. It is only a statement of Christian teaching. It does not have many stories or illustrations. It is simple theology, written for ordinary people.

In many ways the nitty-gritty of church life is in the **local** church, but that is not my theme here. On the other hand it is scarcely possible to write about the 'universal' church without getting involved in the biblical teaching concerning the 'local' church. Readers will notice how when I want to say something about the universal church, as soon as I get down to practicalities, the universal aspect tends to fade out and one finds oneself talking – or writing – about some concrete and local situation. I have not altogether obliterated this tendency from the text of the following chapters, nor have I wanted to, but I feel there is much to be said for considering the whole before the parts. I have deliberately left aside for the moment, as much as I have been able, teaching about the local church in order to focus on the universal church.

As explained in my previous **How To** book all translations are my own but tend to be in a modern 'King James' style.

I am again grateful to friends who have been a stimulus and encouragement to me: the people of Chrisco Fellowship, Nairobi, Kenya, who first heard many of the chapters of this book. Much of it was preached at 'Central Church', 'City Church', and the last chapter was preached in 'KICC Church' all of them Nairobi congregations of the Chrisco Fellowship of Churches. As always I am grateful for the encouragements of my family, and for Chris Mungeam whose enthusiasm keeps me writing for Sovereign World!

Michael Eaton
Nairobi

PART ONE

Introducing the Church

Chapter 1

Is 'Church' Necessary?

Many people who come to Jesus do not move on to enjoy
God's church. It is quite common to find Christians who
are drifters, moving from church to church following the
most interesting preacher, but not very committed to any
congregation at all. They are not interested in 'the
church'. They feel committed to Jesus, but feel 'church' is
another matter altogether and a rather boring subject.
They have not given very much thought to 'the church'.

I was like this myself. I was converted to Jesus, through
the ministry of a young peoples' meeting, just before my
fifteenth birthday. Not long afterwards I decided to start a
little fellowship meeting for myself and a few friends. I
would not have called what we were doing 'church' and it
did not cross my mind to tell the minister of the church I
attended on Sunday evenings anything about what I was
doing. I felt that that was my own business. At that time I
felt I had as much right to start a Bible-study group as I
had to start a chess club or a cycling club (I started those
as well!). I went to church on Sunday evenings because it
was where I met fellow Christians. I would not have felt
that what I was doing was in any way obligatory –
although it was what I wanted to do. On Sunday mornings I had a leisurely laze in bed. Sometimes I might get
up early – or what I thought was early – to visit somewhere where I had heard there was some great preaching!

But of course the Bible's way of talking about 'church' is much more significant than I had realised, and the day came when I realised I had to be more committed to 'church' as part of being committed to Jesus. The truth is, 'the church' is the one and only body of people that is sacred, indispensable for Christian maturity, and an obligatory part of Christian obedience. There is nothing else like it. Think of the various things that a Christian might be involved in. When I was saved I belonged to several libraries; I went to school during weekdays. Later on I went to a college for further education. But none of these are particularly mandatory. None of them are laid down by God as something which is required and obligatory for his people. God does not demand that one attends a library. God does not even demand that one goes to school. There are many people in the world who do not go to school and yet who are not guilty of any kind of disobedience to God!

Even within Christian circles there are many organisations that Christians might attend. One might be in a young peoples' fellowship, another in a women's meeting or young wives' fellowship. He or she might go on to belong to a theological college or a missionary society. But again it must be said that none of these are obligatory. There are churches without any young peoples' meeting. There are groups of churches that do not use theological colleges for their method of training preachers. But no sin is involved in this omission. But 'the church' is in a different category altogether. It is something demanded by God. Jesus said *'I will build my church'* (Matthew 16:18). There is nothing else that comes in this category. He did not demand educational establishments or any sort of club or any particular type of church meeting. But he did say that he was bringing into being his church.

So 'the church' is not an option that one is to be casual about. It is part of the Christian life, part of Christian obedience. One might ask 'Is it possible to be a Christian

9

without going to church?' I suppose it is. But, generally speaking, it is not possible to be an **obedient** or **fruitful** Christian without being committed to some kind of local congregation. And it is not possible to be a **lively** Christian or a **fruitful** Christian without being in some kind of fellowship with other Christian people.

Why is it that there are true Christians who are not very excited about the church? There are many reasons. It may be that for them 'church' is asociated in their minds with something boring, traditional, monotonous, legalistic, ritualistic, powerless. I can sympathise! I never was a very 'religious' person in the way that people normally think of 'religion'. When I discovered Jesus as my Saviour it took a while before I realised that any sort of 'church-going' was needed at all. For some new Christians – and I was one of them – it takes a little time before they realise that 'church' is part of God's plan for their lives.

But there are other reasons. Some do not 'enjoy church' because the congregation they relate to is dull and boring. That is tragic. But lively congregations do exist.

Some might not enjoy church because it speaks to them **more** powerfully than they want it to. The preaching is so relevant that they are uncomfortable. They give all sorts of reasons for not going near a place where God is likely to speak to them.

What about those who **do** 'enjoy the church' but who do not know Jesus at all? It is possible to grow up in the church, to be 'baptised' or dedicated as a baby, to go to the Lord's Supper, to be 'confirmed', even to be ordained as a preacher – but not be a Christian at all. In the Bible (John chapter 3), Nicodemus was a good man, a teacher of the Old Testament, an attender at a place of worship. But he had never known what it was to be 'born again'. Jesus told him that something had to happen to him by the working of the Holy Spirit that would make him a new person altogether. He had to put his faith in Jesus Christ. Yes, it is possible to 'enjoy church' but not have experienced the power of Jesus in one's life at all. The remedy to that is simple: *'Believe on the Lord Jesus Christ and you shall be saved'* (Acts 16:31).

But for the Christian, there are good reasons to make sure that we are truly involved in and enjoying God's church, and that is our concern in the following pages.

In the Bible the word 'church' is used in two main ways. It can refer to the entire people of God. When Jesus said *'I will build my church'* (Matthew 16:18) this was the way in which he was using the word. We call this the 'universal' church. I sometimes speak about the 'worldwide' or 'international' church. This is the entire company of God's people throughout the world.

I have also mentioned 'going to church', which is a very local matter. There might be a Christian fellowship of some kind that meets not very far away from where we live. This is what we mean when we speak of the 'local' church. In thirty-five verses (beginning with Acts 15:41) the Bible speaks of 'churches'. Then it refers to particular congregations of believing Christians.

Years ago I heard a famous preacher say 'The New Testament talks more about churches than it does about the church'. He was suggesting that we ought to concentrate on the local church and not bother about the 'universal church'. The idea was that the universal church only exists in the form of local churches, so we should not bother too much about the 'worldwide' church but just get on with what we should be doing in our local situation. For many years of my life I followed this advice of the famous preacher and concentrated more on the local church than upon the universal church. But I have come to feel that his advice was not as reliable as I thought it was. Actually the Bible has a lot to say about the 'universal' church and most of the picture-language used in connection with the church ('body', 'bride', 'temple', and so on) refers to the entire worldwide church more than it does to the local situation. When Jesus first raised the subject of his church and said to his disciples *'On this rock I will build my church'* he was referring to his total

11

worldwide church. He **began** with the whole church, when he first introduced the word (or its Aramaic equivalent).

One might ask, does it make any difference, which aspect one begins with? I think it does. People who begin with the whole and then get down to the details seem to have a different attitude compared to those who focus on their local situation but rarely lift up their eyes to anything wider. It is easy for us to concentrate on our bit of God's work and think the wider church is only a matter of other people getting on with their work for God as we are getting on with ours! This is actually neglecting the worldwide church altogether! The person with too heavy a 'local church' mentality is often small-minded and unaware of what God is doing in his world. Such people tend to be very traditional and resistant to anything new that God is doing. When they pray for revival they are actually only praying for blessing on what God is currently doing in their circle. When revival comes they normally resist it, though they may have been praying for revival for years! People with a heavily 'local church' mentality do not notice revival when it is taking place a hundred metres away.

We shall **begin** by focusing on the teaching of the Bible concerning the whole worldwide church of God. As much as possible we shall focus on the whole and leave the nitty-gritty of the 'local church' till later. That is important also, but that can wait till another book. We begin by seeing the whole before the parts.

Chapter 2

The Ambition of Jesus

It was Jesus himself who talked about his church. You can't say 'I love Jesus, but I don't love his church'. If you don't love the church, you don't love Jesus. For he loves it. He was the one who Himself announced that his plan for the world involves building his church. The church is people. God created many things in this world, material things, animals, angels. But it is men and women that God loves supremely, and he loves people coming together. His supreme design in this world is to bring together a people. He saves and redeems and rescues and cleans, and so makes his saved and purified people to be 'the church'.

You will never be truly happy and fulfilled unless you relate to the church of Jesus Christ. I know that thousands of 'churches' are thoroughly boring places. Nevertheless, Jesus' purpose for this world revolves around his kingly power, and that royal power of Jesus brings into being his people, the church.

The church is not a 'building', literally. I know we often speak of the 'church' on such-and-such a road, when in fact we are only referring to a building. In the New Testament the word 'church' never means 'church building'. Yet the people of God are **like** a building. Jesus said *'I will **build** my church'* (Matthew 16:18). The people of God are a spiritual building, with a spiritual foundation, with living stones, with a corner-stone, with an inhabitant, and with a distinctive character.

Paul would speak about the church being 'built' on the apostles and prophets and growing into a *'holy temple in the Lord'* (Ephesians 2:20–22). He would say *'You are God's building'* and would use the picture-language of a foundation and of builders, and so on (1 Corinthians 3:10–17).

But it was Jesus who first introduced the idea of the church being like a building. We read about it in Matthew 16:13–20. Jesus was ready to start training his disciples for the future church that He knew was coming into being. He would be the builder and he would use these disciples. So he took them to Caesarea Philippi, and while he was there asked the disciples *'Who do people say that I am?'* The disciples went on to talk about the different views of Jesus that were going around. But it was not enough that the disciples should just be following the average opinion as to who Jesus was. So Jesus went a bit further. *'And who do you say that I am?'* Peter speaks, responding to a question Jesus had asked of **all** the disciples. *'You are the Christ . . . '*.

How does Peter know that Jesus is the Son of God? He is not following the speculations and guesses of outsiders. So how has Peter come to know what he knows? Jesus tells him. *'Blessed are you, Simon Barjona, for flesh and blood did not reveal this to you but my Father who is in heaven.'*

Then Jesus comes to introduce the church. *'And I say to you that you are Peter and upon this Rock I shall build my church, and the gates of death shall not overcome it. I am giving to you the keys of the kingdom of heaven and whatever you bind upon earth shall have been bound in heaven and whatever you loose on earth shall have been loosed in heaven.'*

The Old Testament had spoken of the congregation of Israel. What is new here is that Jesus speaks about himself as personally building **his** congregation.

He is using the picture language of a building. We may pick out several aspects of this spiritual building.

1. It has a foundation. In the picture-language of the New Testament sometimes Jesus is pictured as the foundation of the church (see 1 Corinthians 3:11), and the church is built on him. But sometimes the picture is used differently. Sometimes the foundation is the very first members of the church and consists of apostles and prophets. If the church is pictured as a building of living people, the foundation also consists of people. They were the 'first layer', the 'first floor' of the spiritual building. It is the ones who were in at the beginning that set the character of the church. Others in the church are built on them. The foundation of the entire church of Jesus Christ is the apostles and prophets (see Ephesians 2:20–22). Peter was the very first one of them, and had the privilege of doing the first preaching on the day of Pentecost. *'You are Peter – which means Rock – and upon this rock I shall build my church.'* The church is not built upon Peter in his personal character. Peter was a very erratic person. It is Peter as the first person to confess his faith in Jesus as the Son of God, Peter as the one who received a revelation from the Father, Peter as the leader of the apostles and the one who would stand up and preach on the day of Pentecost.

The church takes its character from its beginnings. If you want to see what the church is, see what it was when God first started with it. God took twelve men. They were weak and frail and often quite foolish. They had silly earthly ambitions and quarrels among themselves about who was the greatest.

But Jesus chose them, and from the very beginning he chose one of them to be a leader within that twelve. He gave him a new name, 'Rocky', which is the meaning of the name 'Peter'. But Peter was far from being rock-like! He was always slipping and sliding and could have been called 'Sandy' rather than 'Rocky'! But Jesus chose to start his church with him and others like him. The church went up on 'the foundation of apostles and prophets'. It means that the church is built upon revelation. Jesus gave these men revelations about himself. The church goes up on the basis of faith. Where there is no faith in Jesus there is no church. It also means that Jesus built the church upon himself, because what Peter did (and others immediately after) was to preach about Jesus.

This is why it is also possible (using the picture-language differently) to say that Jesus is the foundation of the church (as in 1 Corinthians 3:11 and 1 Peter 2:6–8). But the church is not built on **anyone** who spells his name J-E-S-U-S. It is built by the Jesus revealed by the Father, the Jesus who is the object of our faith, Jesus the Son of the living God. The foundation of the church is also the apostles because they were the first members of God's church and the first to preach Jesus. Peter had that privilege in a wonderful way, because he was the first to preach on the day of Pentecost.

2. The church has an owner and a lord. Jesus says *'I will build my church'*. It is not 'You will build your church'. It is not Peter who owns the church. We must not regard it as belonging to any mere human being, however great that person may be. Jesus is the Lord and owner of his church. This is why the church must not be changed or used for our own purposes.

3. The church has a builder. *'I will build my church'*, says Jesus. It is the task of the church to see what Jesus is doing and do it with him. It would have been understandable if Jesus had said 'You will build my church' or 'You are Peter and I will build your church'. But it is not Peter who builds the church. It is Jesus.

4. It has under-builders or servants. Jesus is the supreme builder but under him there are men and women who follow him and do some building with him. Paul says that he is a master-builder and that as he preached about Jesus, he was laying the foundation of the church. Jesus said: You are Peter. I will use you to be the first layer of the church. I will give you the keys of the kingdom. I am going to use you.

5. The church has a destiny. Jesus uses a future tense: *'I will build my church'*. From that point on Jesus was building his church. A few months later He would be risen and ascended. He would be at the Father's right hand and from the Father's throne he would pour out the Holy Spirit upon that little church. He was building his church. And Jesus is building his church still. It is not finished yet!

6. The church has an enemy. When Jesus spoke of the *'gates of hell'*, the Greek word for 'hell' is not *Gehenna*, the place of punishment. It is *Hades*, which is death viewed as if it were a place. The city gates, in the ancient world, were often the place of law-courts, the place where authority was exercised and decisions made and business done. Death is being pictured as a strong city with inhabitants who want to overpower the church and kill it. The church of Jesus has demonic enemies who would like to destroy the church and who constantly attack it. But the 'gates of death' shall not prevail.

7. The church has authority. The church has gates as well! For Peter has keys: the picture is of someone opening doors or gates. *'I am giving to you the keys of the kingdom of heaven . . . '.*

Keys to a city are used to open up and let someone in or to lock and keep someone out. On the day of Pentecost Peter would open the gates of heaven by preaching about Jesus in the power of the Holy Spirit. The 'gates of death' are open and the devil attacks the church. But by preaching and by spiritual weapons we open the gates of the kingdom of heaven. The kingdom of darkness is driven back and overcome.

'Whatever you bind upon earth shall have been bound in heaven and whatever you loose on earth shall have been loosed in heaven.' Binding and loosing refers to the authority the church has to bring about God's will. 'Binding' is not a reference to 'binding Satan' (which would imply that loosing is loosing Satan – an odd idea!). It refers to the church's authority to prevent what is not God's will and to release what is God's will. The church

17

has authority in at least three ways. It has authority to say what is and what is not the truth of God. It has authority to say who are and who are not members of the true church of God, that is, to say what is and what is not the way of salvation. And it has authority to get God's will done for him on earth.

That is the church! Jesus was the one who introduced it to us. You might ask: where is it? It is not any particular denomination or grouping of churches. It is not any particular apostolic circle. It is not any organisation put together by modern church leaders. The church of Jesus Chriat is that visible company of everyone everywhere who believes in Jesus as the Son of God. It consists of everyone who has his life built on Jesus, the Jesus revealed by the apostles and prophets.

Chapter 3

Church and Kingdom

'Kingdom' is a very fashionable word. For some it refers
to getting involved in political issues. For others it is a
reference to doing things in a charismatic style. There
used to be a time when people who talked a lot about
'kingdom' had in mind high morality. For some people,
'kingdom of God' means heaven. For others 'the kingdom' is just another way of saying 'the church'. For some
'kingdom' means the dramatic events that take place in
the world in connection with the second coming of Jesus.

Let us begin by seeing what the 'kingdom' is, and then
how it relates to the church of Jesus. We confine ourselves
to Matthew's gospel.

1. **The reign of God was the main theme of Jesus' ministry.** When Matthew's gospel reports the ministry of John
he summarises John's message in the words *'Repent, for
the reign of God is at hand'* (Matthew 3:2). Similarly
Jesus' message, when he begins to preach in Galilee, is
summarised in the same words (Matthew 4:17). When the
twelve apostles are sent out, their message is also 'The
reign of heaven is at hand' (Matthew 10:7).

The subject-matter of Jesus' preaching is the 'good news
of the reign of God' (Matthew 4:23; 9:35).

2. **God's 'kingdom' is his rule or his reign, more than it is
a place.** You can nearly – but not quite – always substitute
the phrase 'reign of God' whenever you come across the

word 'kingdom'. The 'kingdom' is God himself acting as king. To enter God's 'kingdom' means to experience his reigning and ruling in our lives and in this world. We would do well to translate 'kingdom' by 'reign of God' or 'dominion of God' or 'rule of God', when such a meaning is natural. But secondarily the 'kingdom' is a realm in which a rule or reign is taking place. Matthew's gospel can speak of the 'kingdoms of this world' (Matthew 4:8; also 24:7); in such occurrences the word does refer to a realm in which reigning and ruling is taking place When the rewarded disciple will sit at the table in fellowship with Abraham, Isaac and Jacob in the 'kingdom' of God (Matthew 8:11), 'kingdom' seems to be the final realm in which God reigns.

3. **The reigning and ruling of God is past, present and future.** The reign of God came with Jesus. Jesus is the king. Where the King is, there God is reigning and ruling. Before the coming of Jesus there was no one greater than John the Baptist (Matthew 11:11), yet the least person who has experienced the reign of God in his life through Jesus is in this respect greater than John. The reign has come, because Jesus has come.

It has come in Jesus; but **the kingdom is coming yet more**. This is what was in mind when Jesus spoke of the 'mystery' of the reign of God when he taught his disciples in parables. The first was the parable of the sower which, Jesus said, was the key to all the other parables (Mark 4:13). It was a parable about parables. The remaining six parables all deal with the kingdom.

Jesus speaks of the 'mystery' of the kingdom (Matthew 13:11). A 'mystery' is something that people could never discover by their own cleverness but which God has now revealed to those who have hearts open to hear from God. The Old Testament predicted that one day God's reign would overwhelm and finally remove all earthly reigns of earthly kings (Daniel 2:31–35, 44–45). Matthew 13 tells of the hidden-yet-revealed secret of God. The kingdom has come! It has not yet been completely brought to its final triumph but its impact in the world has started. The first parable is the key to the others. The kingdom has **varied** responses. Although the reign of God is making its way powerfully in the story of this world, yet it is not so powerful that all sin and wickedness have been removed. The kingdom comes with power but it is not irresistible power. Men and women can reject it, or they can receive it and **then** neglect it so that it does not come to the full fruitfulness that it could have come to.

The second parable, concerning the wheat and the tares (Matthew 13:24–40) speaks of the cleansing of the kingdom at the end of the world. The field is the world (not the church!). Those who are experiencing the rule of God, and those who are experiencing the rule of Satan are together in the world. At the end wickedness is cleansed out of the world. The prophecy of Daniel 2 comes to a final conclusion. God's reign sweeps away all rival kingships.

The third and fourth parables (Matthew 13:31–32, 33) speak of the way in which the reign of God, seemingly weak, is in fact powerful and will have vast impact upon the world.

After these parables Jesus leaves, the crowd and goes into a house (Matthew 13:34–36a). Within the house he explains the parable of the wheat and tares (Matthew 13:36b–43).

Then come the parable of the hidden treasure (Matthew 13:44) and the pearl of great price (Matthew 13:45–46) which speak of the demands that the kingdom makes.

A seventh and final parable again stresses separation at the end (Matthew 13:47–50).

A final comment at the end of these parables emphasises that the Christian must understand these realities (Matthew 13:52). The Christian is like a scribe, in the sense of having been taught by Jesus. He knows something of the 'old', the predictions concerning the reign of God. He also knows something of the 'new'. He knows that the reign of God has started in Jesus, and that it is still making its way forcefully in God's world. He knows that one day the reign of God will triumph and evil will be swept away altogether when the King comes in person.

The reign of God has come in Jesus; but it is coming yet more; and it will finally come in great glory. Matthew 7:21 speaks of a **future** entering of the kingdom. *'That day'* (Matthew 7:22) is the final day of judgement and the triumphant reign of God.

4. Now let us consider some **aspects of the reign of God**. Firstly, **the rule of God is a rule of righteousness**. The Sermon on the Mount (Matthew 5–7) is a description of the righteousness that Jesus is asking of his disciples. Mention of the reign of God is prominent. Within that block of teaching (Matthew 5:1–8:1) we first have 'the beatitudes' (Matthew 5:3–12), when a basic description of the godly life is given. In the first and last beatitude the blessing upon the godly people described is 'Theirs is the reign of God' (Matthew 5:3, 10). When the disciple prays, he should pray that God's rule will come in this world (Matthew 6:10). It is the rule of God and its righteousness which he seeks above all else (Matthew 6:33).

The disciples once enquired about who would be the greatest in Jesus' new regime (Matthew 18:1). Jesus replied to the effect that experiencing God's rule in our lives involves child-like simplicity (Matthew 18:3, 4; 19:14). Later he said that the *'rule of God'* (Matthew 18:23) involved a radical attitude of forgiveness (Matthew 18:23–35).

On another occasion when the question is asked about status in the coming rule of Jesus (Matthew 20:21), Jesus makes it clear that ambition will have to be purified and that suffering and sacrificial humility will be involved (Matthew 20:22–28).

Another way of putting the same point is to say that to experience **the reigning and ruling of God in our lives requires much dedication**. In Matthew's gospel and else-where we learn of the demand of the reign of God. When Jesus says *'Repent, for the reign of God is at hand'*

(Matthew 3:2), the point is that also the reign of God in our lives is *'at hand'* in the person of Jesus. We shall not experience that powerful activity of God reigning in our lives, unless we on our side are ready to change our entire attitude towards God, to 'repent'. Jesus' rule is not inherited unless the godly life of the Beatitudes and the Sermon on the Mount is actually lived. By living upon the instruction of Jesus the disciples must exceed the righteousness of the scribe or Pharisee. Otherwise he will not experience the rule of God (Matthew 5:20). If his life or his ministry disparages or loosens any detail of the law (before it has been fulfilled by Jesus) he will be least in the reign of God. His experience of God's kingship in his life will be diminished (Matthew 5:19).

Membership does not come by physical descent. Jewish people may be 'sons of the kingdom' by virtue of their nationality, but without faith they will, says Jesus, be thrown into the outer darkness (Matthew 8:12). Because of their unbelief the rule of God which had before been seen supremely in Israel would be taken away from Israel (Matthew 21:43). The rule of God in our lives does not come by inherited tratitional religion. It comes by repentance and faith. When there is repentance and faith, swindling tax-collectors and immoral women come to experience the rule of God in their lives (Matthew 21:31) more than chief priest and elders (Matthew 21:23–32). The parable of Matthew 22:2–14 again begins *'The rule of God is like . . . '*, and goes on to explain how it was offered to Israel first, but Israel rejected the demand for faith. Now the kingdom is on offer for *'both good and bad'* (Matthew 22:10).

What the reign of God requires is bold, energetic faith, and drastic action. Matthew 11:12 is a difficult verse to translate and understand but it is probably a helpful verse in this connection. It may be translated *'From the days of John the Baptist until now the reign of heaven makes its way powerfully and aggressive people seize it'*. The ministry of John the Baptist was the starting-point. He prepared the way for Jesus. Then Jesus received the anointing of the Spirit and from that point onwards John's ministry was at an end. He immediately decreased (see John 3:30). Soon he was in prison (Matthew 11:2). He heard about the ministry of Jesus but took no part in it. Yet his ministry was the dividing line between two ages of time. It was from the end of John's ministry onwards that the reign of God was powerfully manifested in the mighty works of Jesus (see Matthew 11:4–5).

Matthew 11:12 has been taken to refer to the violence that the kingdom **suffers** from people like Herod. There is a Greek word here which could be translated 'makes its way aggressively' or 'suffers violence'. Some translate *'The kingdom of God suffers violence ... '*.

But I doubt whether 'suffering violence' is relevant, because the royal activity of God is not in itself directly able to 'suffer violence' at the hands of Herod or anyone else.

A similar view, accepting a similar translation, takes it that the kingdom of heaven is forcibly seized **by its friends**, but there does not seem very strong evidence that it should be taken this way.

I prefer to translate *'From the days of John the Baptist until now the kingdom of heaven makes its way powerfully* (an allusion to the signs of Matthew 11:4, 5) *and aggressive people seize it'* (in contrast to the stumbling mentioned in Matthew 11:6). *'People of violence'* is a play on words and has a good meaning. It refers to aggressive faith, which actually John has not been exhibiting in asking the question he had asked according to Matthew 11:3.

The idea then is: the kingdom of God acts powerfully and requires a powerful response. This fits the constant theme of the gospels that the kingdom demands violent action: hating father and mother, enduring not peace but a sword, being willing to surrender everything for the sake of experiencing God's rule, and so on. Some even remain single as *'eunuchs for the sake of the reign of God'* (Matthew 19:12).

This view also fits Luke 16:16 where 'forces his way' obviously has a good meaning. *'The law and the prophets prophesy until John. From then on the kingdom of God is preached-as-good-news and every one forces his way into it.'* If we take Matthew any other way than the one I have suggested, Luke changed the meaning!

Another saying which speaks of the single-mindedness of the kingdom is Matthew 12:25, 26. When Jesus says *'every rule divided against itself is laid waste ... if Satan casts out Satan ... how can his rule stand?'* (Matthew 12:25, 26), he is using a piece of logical argumentation, but it also suggests that the reign of God is not divided against itself. God's reign and rule is single-minded in pursuing the aim of subjecting the world to God himself. Wealth is so preoccupying that it blocks our experience of the kingdom of God unless God powerfully works to do the impossible (Matthew 19:23–26).

The reign of God requires constant readiness. The rule of God is like a wedding when you do not quite know when the bridegroom will arrive. (Punctuality was not worshipped in the way in which it is in the modern western world!) So the assistants of the wedding have to be ready all the time (Matthew 25:1–13). The next parable (Matthew 25:14–30) obviously makes a similar point.

In all of this it is the present, this-world, fact of God's reign that is in mind. Yet the demand of the kingdom relates to the final kingdom also. *'That day'* in Matthew 7:22 is the final day of judgement. Only those who have lived a godly life will enter into the final blessings of the kingdom (Matthew 7:21). At a final day of judgement some but not others will *'inherit the reign of God'* in a way that others will not (Matthew 25:34). In that day there will be fellowship with Jesus in a way that surpasses what has ever been known. We shall feast with Jesus in His father's kingdom (Matthew 26:29). There is rich fellowship where God is acting as king. The final reign of God will be the experience of a warm-hearted brotherhood. The rewarded disciple will sit at the table in fellowship with Abraham, Isaac and Jacob in the kingdom of God (Matthew 8:11).

Consider next the **grace of God's kingdom**. The fact that the reign of God is demanding does not mean that we earn it or deserve it. The point of the parable of Matthew 20:1–11 is that the rewards of God are gracious and surprising. The theme is that of the 'reward' of the kingdom (as is clear from Matthew 19:27–30). Jesus tells his enquiring disciples a parable that lets them know that some thought worthy of reward will not get what they think they deserve. Some who come in at the last hour get as much as those who are long-standing disciples. Jesus sovereignly and graciously bestows his blessings of the kingdom as he sees fit. The rule of God is gracious. It requires repentance but its progress is hindered by legalism. The scribes and Pharisees *'closed up the rule of God among people'* by their regulations (Matthew 23:13).

5. We are now ready, then, to see how 'church' and 'kingdom' relate to each other. The two ideas are different, yet a 'kingdom' way of looking at the Christian faith will enable us to see what salvation is. It is not 'going to church', although that is good and right, as I am maintaining in this book. It is not doctrinal head-knowledge, although to understand God's Word is a great privilege. It is not to have a theoretical understanding of justification by faith. To be 'saved' is none of these things. **Salvation is experiencing the reign of God.** It is when the power of God's Holy Spirit is at work in one's life. Unless you are born from above, Jesus said, you will not *'enter the kingdom'*. This is what salvation is: entering the kingdom, coming under the mighty activities of God's Holy Spirit. It is when God by his Holy Spirit illuminates our minds, gives us faith, changes our hearts, redirects our motives, gives us an appetite for godliness and holiness, opens our mouth in confession and praise.

A 'kingdom' way of looking at the Christian faith will enable us to keep away from denominational jealousy and 'empire-building'. Where Christians are preoccupied with their own local church and others in the same pattern of ministry, it seems invariably to lead to traditionalism, preoccupation with one's own denomination or five-fold ministry or whatever our circle of churches might like to call itself. It seems to lead to 'sheep-stealing' from other Christian churches and a separation from other Christian fellowships nearby. But what matters is the reign of God! What matters is how and where God is acting in power and sovereignty. It is at this point that it is important to see that 'kingdom' is not 'church'. Jesus talked about his church (Matthew 16:18) but his message was not 'Repent, for the church is at hand'; it was *'Repent for the kingdom is at hand'*. The 'kingdom of God' does not simply mean 'the Christians' or 'the church'. The church preached the kingdom of God, but it was not preaching about itself.

The kingdom – the royal activity of God – brings the church into being. As Jesus went through the villages of Israel his royal power was bringing the community of the disciples into being. Today, we only see the church of Jesus built up as God works powerfully through his people. All evangelism is power-evangelism. The church comes into being not through man-made cleverness or wisdom or even through 'church growth' strategies (which seem to **observe** growth in others rather than create it themselves). The royal power of God creates the church!

The kingdom – the royal activity of God – uses the church as its channel of influence out into the world. There was a time when the reign of God used Israel as its means of ministering to the world. Israel was to be the light to enlighten the gentiles. But now the kingdom has been taken from Israel and given to the church. It does not mean that there is no possibility of Israel's being saved – far from it – but it means that God's way of reaching people and extending the kingdom's influence is through using the church.

The kingdom – the royal activity of God – is seen in the life of the church. We live the life of the kingdom. The life of God becomes visible in us. Men and women see our good works and glorify our Father who is in heaven. The church is the fellowship of those who have experienced the power of God's reign in their lives.

The kingdom – the royal activity of God – is seen in the ministry of the church. The church has the keys of the kingdom. It binds and looses. It brings about that which is God's will and prevents that which is not God's will. The keys of the kingdom are placed within the hands of people. It is we who proclaim good news, forbid entrance to the unsaved, urge conversion, and bear witness to what God has done in our lives.

Chapter 4

Church and Israel

The relationship between the church and the nation of Israel is a vital matter for several reasons. It affects how we read the Old Testament. Are 'Israel' and 'church' identical? Can we take the many promises of the Old Testament and apply them to ourselves? Or must we regard them as applying to Israel and **not** to us directly. If we see a **lot** of national Israel in the Old Testament but **little** of the church in the Old Testament it will affect our mentality as we look out on God's world, and we shall be very preoccupied with the politics of modern Israel.

There are a number of different approaches that Christians have adopted towards the subject and it may help us if we list some of them before I try to present what I think is the biblical teaching.

1. There is **the approach that totally identifies Israel and the church**. It takes 'Israel' in the Old Testament to be simply a symbol for the church and does not give any attention to the nation of Israel at all. I do not think this is truly biblical. It is true that Israel is a picture of the church in many ways, for the church of Jesus is a 'holy nation'. Yet one cannot simply treat the nation of Israel as a picture of the church and nothing more. This is often put as if there were one great 'covenant' flowing through the story of Israel–church. But this is a mistake in my opinion. There are immense contrasts between the

29

'covenant of law' (made in the days of Moses) and the other covenants. In the covenant of law, people take an oath (which is what is happening in Exodus 19:8). In covenants of generosity, God takes an oath (see Genesis 22:16; Psalm 89:35; Hebrews 6:16–18). The contrasts between Mosaic law and covenants of grace are great. The Bible never puts covenants of law and grace all into one big covenant.

2. There is an approach totally opposite to the one just mentioned, in which **Israel and the church are viewed as two totally different entities**. Christians who accept this view tend to be very 'pro-Israel', tend to be unsympathetic towards Arabs (many of whom are Christians), and tend to give support to Israeli political conduct without adequately considering its justice or injustice. They talk as if God has two purposes for two separate peoples.

3. An even greater extreme is **the 'two ways of salvation' approach**. Some have spoken and written as if there is a way of salvation for Judaism and a different way of salvation for gentiles. No one who really believes the Bible can accept this. There is only one way of salvation. People in Israel can be saved only 'if they do not continue in unbelief' (Romans 11:23).

We need to find the biblical balance and the precise way these things are put to us in the Scriptures.

1. **Great illumination comes if one understands Romans 9:6**. The word 'Israel' has two meanings, both of which are found in Romans 9:6b. It may refer to the nation (as in the second time 'Israel' comes in Romans 9:6). It may refer to God's truly believing people (as in the first time the word 'Israel' is used in this verse). Not all who are 'Israel' (God's truly saved people) are from Israel (that is, from the earthly nation).

True Israel consists of those who believe in the promises of God concerning Jesus, the seed of Abraham. The phrases *'seed of Abraham'* or *'children of Abraham'* also may refer to physical descendants of Abraham (see Romans 11:1), or to those who share Abraham's faith

(Galatians 3:29). This was Jesus' point in John chapter 8. *'We are Abraham's seed'* said the Jewish people (John 8:33). Jesus said *'Well, in one sense you are Abraham's seed* (John 8:37) *yet if you were really Abraham's seed you would do what Abraham did'* (John 8:39–41).

'Israel' is first of all a spiritual term. Then secondly it becomes a national term. Romans 9:6 says *'Not all are Israel who are of Israel'*. This means 'Not all are God's truly-saved-Israel, simply because they physically descend from the nation of Israel. It can be seen that the word 'Israel' has two meanings. There is 'truly-saved-Israel' and there is 'national-Israel'.

2. We need to understand the teaching concerning 'the remnant'. As the story of the nation of Israel went on 'true Israel' became a remnant within national Israel. There was a *'remnant according to grace'* (Romans 11:5). At Pentecost the blessings of God came upon the remnant, true believers, all of whom were Jews. The new covenant was made with the nation of Israel – reduced to a remnant. Jeremiah chapter 31 says that God took the nation of Israel out of Egypt and gave them a covenant through Moses. But they broke it (Jeremiah 31:32). Yet God promised that he would make a new covenant with the house of Israel. This is literally true. The new covenant – that all Christians have a share in – was made with the 'house of Israel'. All of the Christians on the day of Pentecost were Jews. God made a new covenant with the house of Israel reduced to a remnant.

3. Then **Christian gentiles were grafted into remnant-Israel**. This is how it comes about that gentile Christians are part of God's true Israel. The true people of God were within the nation of Israel. They were reduced and reduced over the centuries until they were a tiny remnant. They were enlarged and further enlarged by the coming in of many gentiles. The church is remnant-Israel plus gentiles added into it.

In this sense one may say that true Israel is the church, but one has to remember exactly how this comes about. It is not simply that 'Israel is the church' in some over-simple manner. It is rather that God's true people were originally all Jewish. Now God's people has been enlarged by the coming in of millions of gentiles. God's church is remnant-Israel with gentile believers grafted into it

4. National-Israel still exists and Scripture teaches that **one day there will be a spiritual awakening in national Israel** and the nation as a whole will turn to Jesus and so be grafted back into the true Israel! This is a very surprising turn of events. No wonder Paul speaks of *'this mystery'* (Romans 11:25–27)!

So the promises of God to Abraham and his seed apply to all Christians. There is only one people of God. At one stage the people of God were a nation. Then they were a remnant within a nation. Then there came a point where Israel as God's people in the form of a nation came to an end. *'The kingdom of God will be taken away from you'*, said Jesus to the leaders of Israel, *'and it will be given to a nation producing the fruits of it'*. The people of God would cease to be totally identified with the nation of Israel. The Jewish leaders would lose their authority. The church would be re-formed and re-structured with remnant-Israel as its foundation. Upon that basis Jesus will build his church. It will be a renewed nation *'producing the fruits'* of the kingdom of God, and no longer identified with national Israel. Although remnant-Israel is the starting point of the church, Jews and gentiles are grafted into it and within the church of Jesus there is now neither Jew nor Greek (Galatians 3:28).

However it must be noted that remnant-Israel is the starting point of this renewed nation, the church. And the promise stands that Israel will one day experience spiritual awakening and so in this way come into the new nation, the church.

The word 'church' starts to be used after Jesus has come, and especially after the people of God have received the Holy Spirit in fullness. It was at first remnant-Israel, but soon had gentiles added to it. 'Israel' is the church in its earliest history. 'Church' is Israel in its latest stage. Generally we use the word 'Israel' either of the nation or of God's godly people within the nation. Generally we use the word 'church' for the form that the people of God took after the day of Pentecost. But it must be remembered; there is only one people of God! We Christians are a recent stage in the story that began with 'Israel'. Abraham as a model believer is our spiritual ancestor.

There is only one way of salvation. There is no way of salvation other than by faith in Jesus, Israel's Saviour. There should never be Jewish and gentile sections in the church of Jesus Christ. In his church, Jesus has broken down the dividing wall between Jew and gentile. The church is the expanded form of remnant-Israel; one day the nation of Israel will join us. 'O, the depth of the riches of the wisdom and knowledge of God!'

Chapter 5

Church and State

How should 'the church' relate to the state? To society? To
political reform? Some preachers avoid any involvement
at all with what is going on in their nation. Some years
ago when I preached in old-style South Africa I would be
told I was being 'political' if I said I wanted to see people
of every skin-colour converted to Jesus Christ. Some
preachers like to keep to evangelistic preaching and to
building up the people of God in lives of godliness. Others
try to be preacher-politicians (but as a result are neither
preachers nor politicians!). They talk about agriculture
and prison reform and national morality and make sly
digs at politicians week by week. On Sunday mornings
they denounce the government for its weaknesses and
corruptions, but this does not help anybody. Most of the
congregation are unsaved anyway, and they are quite
happy to have sermons which denounce other people! A
congregation with many unsaved people likes that kind of
preaching, but people have to go elsewhere to find salvation in Jesus! Such preachers like to get notoriety and are
pleased when they find themselves mentioned in the newspaper, but they are embarrassed when someone says to
them 'I want to get saved'.

We must start with the teaching of the Bible. How
should the church relate to the state so far as we can tell
from the Bible? I have the entire church of Jesus Christ in

34

mind. For there are many parts of the world where the church of Jesus is flourishing and the question of how to relate to the state is an important one. In one country the president is truly Christian but there is a powerful Moslem presence. In another country there is a Buddhist establishment and Christians find themselves a strong but persecuted minority. In another country there is a 'state church' but the gospel of Jesus seems to be dying and people in their hundreds are leaving older denominations every day. The lively Christians are not in the 'state church'. The situations in different parts of the world are varied. There do not seem to be many places outside of Europe where there are 'state churches', but even this is a possibility. In one country a Christian president announces 'Our country is a Christian country!' So shortly afterwards Christians agitate for a 'chapel' to be built in State House for daily Christian worship but are disappointed when their Christian president says 'no'. In another country a Christian politician comes to me and says 'I have been asked to be guest of honour at a social welfare meeting, as a member of parliament for the district. But the organisation is a Moslem one. Should I refuse to attend because it is Moslem? They are in my constituency and they are doing a lot of good for the area. What should I do? I am their member of parliament.'

How should the church relate to the state? Let us approach the matter in historical order.

1. **In ancient paganism 'religion' and 'state' were totally identified.** Each country had its own religion. Everyone in the nation had to belong to it. The king was a religious official and expected to be obeyed when he told the people what their faith should be. Think of the story of Daniel chapter 3. Nebuchadnezzar builds an image and demands that his people make it their 'state religion' (Daniel 3:1). He calls the various civic authorities (Daniel 3:2) but he is not enquiring about how they do their 'secular' work; he is demanding that they profess allegiance to his new idol. This leads to persecution. Anyone who does not fall down

35

and worship the state's religion is to be thrown into the fiery furnace (Daniel 3:6). This is a typical pagan state-religion which persecutes anyone who does not follow it.

2. **In ancient Israel 'religion' and 'state' were two aspects of the same people.** Israelite faith used the state machinery to get its support. When Ahab and Jezebel made Baal-worship the 'state-religion' and began to kill God's prophets (1 Kings 18:4), Elijah did something about it and executed the prophets of Baal (1 Kings 18:40). He replaced one persecuting state-religion with another perse-cuting state-religion – the true one! All Israelite wars were 'holy wars' (see 1 Samuel 4:4; 17:45). The king had to profess Israel's faith and uphold it (Deuteronomy 17:14). Religion was a territorial matter. No foreign religion was to be allowed in Israel. When Ruth said *'Your people shall be my people'*, she had also to say *'Your God will be my God'*. Religion and citizenship went together. If you changed religion you might immigrate to where that faith was practised (see 2 Chronicles 11:14). 'One nation, one religion' was the rule of the day everywhere – including in Israel!

3. **The great change was introduced by Jesus.** Jesus did a very surprising thing when he spoke of church and state as two entities. They came to him on one occasion asking *'Shall we pay taxes to Caesar?'* It was a very tricky ques-tion on the understanding that one state should allow only one religion. If Jesus said 'Yes' he was allowing Caesar's authority and therefore Caesar's religion. If he said 'No' he was upholding the state-religion of Israel and obeying Deuteronomy 17:14 but would be in trouble with the Roman authorities.

Jesus did a very remarkable thing. For the first time ever in the history of the world he separated the claims of the state and the claims of faith. He talked of the two not as **one** realm, but as **two** realms: the realm of Caesar and the realm of faith in the God of Israel. *'Render to Caesar the things that are Caesar's and to God the things that are*

God's'. It was a startling innovation. From that point on no one ever dared ask him a question (Matthew 22:46)!

Church and state are to be distinct in our thinking. **They have distinct memberships**. The membership of a state is all the people living in that area. The membership of the church is the company of the saved.

They have distinct beginnings. Membership of the state comes at birth; membership of the church comes at new birth and salvation.

They have different weapons. The state may use the sword (Romans 13:4). The weapons of our warfare are not carnal (2 Corinthians 10:3–4).

They have different functions. The state upholds peaceable life for all its citizens. The church's task is to preach and apply the gospel.

They have distinct officials. The church has elders and apostles and deacons and suchlike. The state has members of parliament and politicians and magistrates. The government officials have no status within the church. The church pastors have no status within the government.

They have a different mainstream life. The church may not take upon itself civic functions. The state may not interfere in the mainstream life of the church.

4. **Let us consider now the change introduced by Constantine.** In the year AD 312 the Roman emperor made the Christian faith a state-religion. It was a disastrous change from what Jesus had said and done in Matthew 22. Many Christians were delighted but actually its impact was dreadful. It seemed to be a good idea at first. Taxes was raised to pay the 'clergy'. Buildings were sometimes paid for by public funds. Sunday became a national holiday. But then it became too easy to become a 'Christian'. The gospel became a 'territorial' religion. Infant baptism was practised and everyone was thought to be Christian as soon as they were born. Non-Christians began to be persecuted and even other Christians who did not agree with the 'state-Christians' also were persecuted. Wars became 'holy' wars, as in medieval 'crusades'.

Pastors became state officials. The state often had some control over the church's pastors. Rulers regarded themselves as head of the church in their area. The idea af a state-church was a disastrous move away from the New Testament.

5. **Since the days of Constantine there have been four main ways in which the church and the state have related.**

One way is the way of **hostility**. The state persecutes church. The church tends to despise the state. This is obviously not right.

Another way is that **the church and the state are one but the religious leaders are more powerful than the political leaders**. This is what the Roman Catholic church has always wanted. In 'Catholic Europe' before the 16th century, the church had to confirm the appointment of the kings before they could rule.

Another approach is that **the church and the state are one but the 'secular' leaders are more powerful than the 'religions leaders'**. The English king or queen calls himself or herself head of the church of England. Anglican bishops are chosen in consultation with the British parliament.

A fourth approach is the biblical one, I believe. **I call it 'friendly separatism'**. The church and state are regarded as distinct. Freedom is given for a plurality of faiths in any one state. The gospel does not claim to be a state-religion. It upholds freedom of conscience. The church wants people to come voluntarily to faith. The church wants to resist Moslem-type state-religion where no freedom is given for people to come to faith voluntarily and without persecution. It gives to the state obedience (Romans 13:1), recognition (Romans 13:1b–2) and honour (Romans 13:7). It wants to be salt and light in every nation (Matthew 5:13–16). It is happy for its members to take part in civic affairs, but it does not want state-religion or a religious 'establishment'. It is not abandoning the state to the devil but it wants the state **distinctly** and directly to be under God. It does not want secular state-religion or state-unbelief. State-unbelief is as much tyrannical as state-religion. Countries like the United States of America that pioneered a true and biblical doctrine of church and state now tend to be discriminating against Christians and upholding state-supported agnosticism. That is as much a religious 'establishment' as any other state-religion. The church of Jesus Christ wants freedom for all and freedom for itself. It wants no tyranny of religion over anyone. The church expounds the Scriptures to the state when required or asked to do so, but it does not become a state department, and it has no weapons other than the Word of God and prayer. It contributes to the life of the state via its message and via its members but the church never becomes a state department and never becomes a lord over the state. The church wants to render to Caesar the things that are Caesar's and to God the things that are God's.

Chapter 6

The Church and the Churches

To begin with 'the church' was a single congregation. For the first eight chapters in the book of Acts 'the church' means the church of Jerusalem (Acts 5:11; 7:38; 8:1, 3). No other group of Christians were calling themselves 'the church'. The Christians at Damascus mentioned in Acts 9:1–2 are not called 'the church', and seem to have been a few scattered Christians who had fled from Jerusalem. Acts 9:19 does not say Paul went to 'the church' at Damascus. It seems that at this stage everyone belonged to 'the church' in Jerusalem.

Acts 9:31 is a turning point. The correct text says *'Then the church throughout all Judea, Galilee and Samaria had peace and were built up.'* The Authorised Version follows inferior manuscripts when it reads 'churches'. The best texts have 'church', not 'churches'. Yet the word is used in an unusual way and one can understand why the early scribes changed the word from 'church' to 'churches'. This is the only place where 'church' is used of a large area. Normally 'church' is used either of the whole church everywhere or of a particular congregation. It is never used of an 'area-church' or the 'church of an entire province'. For example, Galatia was a large province but Paul does not speak of the 'church' of Galatia; he speaks of the 'churches' of Galatia (Galatians 1:2).

The explanation seems to be this. Before Acts 9:31 we

read of 'the church' but after Acts 9:31 we read of the churches. There is the congregation of Jerusalem (Acts 11:22; 12:1, 5; 15:4, 22; 18:22) and of Antioch (Acts 11:26; 13:1; 14:27; 15:3). In Acts 14:23 for the first time we find the phrase 'every church'. New congregations had been formed in the cities (see also Acts 15:41; 16:5). Then in Acts 20:17 we read of the church at Ephesus. Acts 9:31 is the turning-point. It probably means 'the church' **of Jerusalem** was now scattered throughout the three provinces. From this point onwards mention is made of 'the churches' of Judea (1 Thessalonians 2:14; Galatians 1:22), never again of 'the church' in Judea. 'The church' of Jerusalem became 'the churches' of the Mediterranean area.

So the question arises: what is the relationship between 'the church' (the entire company of believing people) and 'the churches' (particular congregations in particular places)?

It is interesting to find that some people deny the universal church altogether, and others deny the local church altogether. Robert Banks wants virtually to deny the existence of the universal church, visible on earth.[1] Martyn Lloyd-Jones held a similar view.[2] I have known others who seem to deny the local church altogether. Only recently, as I was preaching in western Kenya, I came across a group of Christians who seemed to be parasites on many local churches but who would not give support or loyalty to any local church, nor would they found their own. 'Local church is a bondage', they said. 'Only the universal church matters'. They had picked the idea up from a Christian leader who did not go to any local church at all. His disciples would travel around the area preaching but forming no congregations. They would sometimes visit local churches but would then leave the local congregation if the ministers began to press upon them the need of commitment to a local congregation. They were trying to deny the necessity of local churches, yet could not survive that way themselves without being parasites on local churches.

But the truth is that both of these emphases are needed in the Christian life. **Both universal church and local church are important, and in that order!** If you only believe in the universal church you become undisciplined. Nothing you do flows into any structure. It fades away rapidly. If your work survives it is only because of friendly local churches in which you exist as a parasite. Something similar is true of what are called 'para-church' organisations (organisations and missions which work with particular ministries, young people's movements, missionary societies, relief agencies and the like). They can be part of the church and have vital ministries, but also they can become rivals to the churches.

On the other hand if you are preoccupied with the local church and ignore the world-wide, international aspect of God's people you become narrow, sectarian, even cultic. You cease to learn anything new from God's Word. Your convictions do not get tested among the wider fellowship of God's people. As God's international church grows and experiences further blessing you get left behind.

The New Testament approach is to keep an equal balance on the universal and the local. Jesus has only one church. All over the world God's Spirit is moving. The only question is where and with whom. We have to keep our eye on everything God is doing so far as it can be done, and yet at the same time we have a part to play in our locality.

It is perhaps at this point that I ought to say something about church government. Over the years there have evolved three major systems of church government: (i) there may be congregations in a given area ruled by a 'bishop' (episcopacy), or (ii) congregations ruled by committees or councils of elders (presbyterianism), or (iii) congregations not ruled by any power outside the congregation itself (congregationalism).

Historically, Roman Catholicism, Anglicanism and others have been ruled by 'bishops'. They are 'episcopal' or 'episcopalian'.

Most churches that have evolved from a missionary organisation are (whether they know it or not) presbyterian in church-government, although they may not use the word 'presbyterian' in their name.

'Baptist' churches, 'Congregational' churches, 'Brethren' chapels and others are 'congregational' in their church government although they may not have the word 'congregational' in their name.

What is in the New Testament? To answer that question in a few dogmatic sentences would be simplistic, but I can express my opinion. It seems to me (i) that there are movements of the Spirit within the story of the Christian church, (ii) movements of the Spirit need the five-fold ministry of apostles, prophets, evangelists, pastors, and teachers. (iii) The New Testament is roughly 'congregational' in the sense that one congregation does not rule in the affairs of another congregation. Yet (iv), and this is vital, there is what I call a 'Holy Spirit presbyterianism'. I have no interest in **organisational** presbyterianism, rule by committees! But there is what I think could be called a 'Holy Spirit presbyterianism'. Congregations in the New Testament do work together but they do so by the leading of the Spirit more than by management by committees, synods or general assemblies.

As the New Testament church grew various groupings of Christians came to have distinct identities. You could say the first 'denominations' arose, but they were more movements of the Holy Spirit. Only when they became hard and cold did they become inflexible 'denominations'. First of all you had the Hebrew-speaking Christians of Jerusalem. They had a distinct identity (see Acts 6:1). They continued until the second century. It comes as a surprise to discover that 'Jerusalem-Christians' did not feel they should witness to gentiles (see Acts 11:19)!

Then something new happened. One day someone *'began to speak to Greeks also'* (Acts 11:20). God blessed them and in no time at all there was a great movement of the Holy Spirit. Thousands of gentiles began to be saved.

Within a few months there was a new movement of the Holy Spirit in the church of Jesus Christ, a 'second wave'.

It led to all sorts of difficulties. The Jerusalem Christians were often troubled that these gentile Christians did not become Jews. Paul became the great missionary and teacher of the gentile Christians, the 'apostle to the gentiles'. People did not always appreciate Paul's teaching. He made it very clear that these gentiles were not under the Mosaic law. Jesus was enough to save them and to sanctify them. What is the relation of 'the church' to 'the churches'? In New Testament times they did not form denominational hierarchies. There was a minimum of organisation, as much as was needed but no more. There was no attempt at centralisation in a Jerusalem headquarters. Each movement of the Spirit as much as possible stayed in touch with what was happening elsewhere. They visited each other, sent letters to each other, and so on. Acts 15 is the story of how two movements of the Spirit met together to clear up a difference between them. The churches had spiritual unity in Christ and yet different circles of apostolic ministry. They shared ministries. Paul and Cephas and Apollos all had influence at Corinth. Paul's ministry at Ephesus later gave way to John's ministry there. The churches recognised that what Jesus was revealing was relevant to all of the churches.

It was an amazing balance of unity and variety. When the Spirit is poured out in power it happens again. The church becomes infinitely varied yet stays together in love under apostolic ministries, listening and obeying what the Spirit says to the churches.

Endnotes

1. See Robert Banks, *Paul's Idea of Community* (Eerdmans, 1980), throughout.
2. See D.M. Lloyd-Jones, *Knowing the Times* (Banner, 1989), p. 193.

PART TWO

The Character of the Church

Chapter 7

The Bride of Christ

The New Testament uses various images or pictures to illustrate the nature of the church. There are dozens of ways the church is pictured in the Bible. It is the salt of the earth, the light of the world, a letter from Christ. It is one loaf, it is the branches of a vine or it is the vineyard itself. It is a pillar, a mother, and so on. There are about a hundred or so of such pictures of the people of God in the Bible, or even more. We have thought already of the church as being like a building (chapter 2 above).

God compares the church also to a bride. Just as a husband guides and supports and cherishes his wife, so Jesus is the head of his worldwide church and guides and supports and provides for her every need. This language is found in the Old Testament: *'Your Maker is your husband'* (Isaiah 54:5); *'as the bridegroom rejoices over the bride, so shall your God rejoice over you'* (Isaiah 62:5).

What is the meaning of this picture language?

1. **On Jesus' side it is love**. He has not dealt with us as our sins deserve. He was the one who took the first steps towards his church. We never would have been saved and rescued, forgiven and delivered, if it were not for him and his love. The church is the bride who has been loved by Christ. All his dealings with us have been full of wisdom.

46

He has been gentle with us, patient towards us. His words have not been unkind or harsh.

His love was costly love. As the Son of God died upon the cross for us, he felt everything that we would have felt. The nails hurt him in the same way that they would have hurt us. The acute suffering and embarrassment of hanging naked upon the cross caused him distress as it would have caused us distress. So determined was the Son of God to have his heavenly bride, he was willing to pay any price to get her.

2. **On our side it is responsiveness**. What does a husband want more than anything in a wife. Is it good looks? No. The one you love is always beautiful to you. Is it great ability? No. What does a lover want more than anything else? Responsiveness. A feeling of rapport. He wants things to be such that at the raising of an eye-brow his loved one smiles back at him. Jesus wants us for ourselves. Putting it practically, Jesus wants our companionship, our talking to him, our sharing with him. The church which is Jesus' bride is the praying, worshipping, loving, responding, people of God. The bride who loves to hear his every word. The bride who loves to be near him.

3. **On Jesus' side it is headship**. Jesus takes the initiative with his church. The church did not decide to love Jesus. Jesus decided to love her. He took the first step. In most cultures of the world it is this way. In a courtship the man acts before the woman – most of the time! So it was with Jesus. *'Christ loved the church'.* He took the first step towards us and came and took us to be his bride.

He was the head and leader in finding us in the first place. He goes on that way. Jesus is the one who leads his church; the church does not lead Jesus. It means that Jesus has ideas for his church. He has things on his heart that he intends doing with and for the church.

4. **On our side it speaks of submission**. If Jesus guides the church in tender love, you as part of Jesus' church respond back toward Jesus. The task of church leaders is to respond to Jesus! The church submits. She lovingly

allows Jesus the heavenly bridegroom to lead her into all of his intentions for her.

What does it mean in practice that Jesus is the head of the church? It means that the church has to find out the will of Jesus for her life. This is to be done at a large-scale level and at a small-scale level. The church is to look to her heavenly Lord and find out what he is doing, and then she is to do it with him. She is to be the helpmate of her heavenly bridegroom.

What is the alternative? If the church is **not** living under the leadership of Jesus, what is she living under instead? The answer is that for much of the time the church seems to be living under human logic and human abilities and customs. Many particular congregations are living under tradition or under some church committee with its intelligent and well-researched techniques. Some churches are under business management techniques of 'goals and strategies'. I cannot altogether criticise that; I suppose the leadership of Jesus can be said to be a goal or a strategy. But I fear that for much of the time there is something carnal and unspiritual about the way 'goals and strategies' are pursued. Where God is moving with power and numbers are expanding, it has not been through managerial technique. It has come through the heavenly Lover acting in power and his bride the church responding in love. Jesus' church is being led by Jesus her heavenly lover. Jesus may allow things and be doing things that would never come into the mind of any church management board. Jesus may decide that part of his church needs a little persecution. Imagine a denominational gathering making that its main recommendation at its general assembly!

5. **On Jesus' side it is purification**. He loves his bride but her state is such that she needs a good deal of cleansing before she is ready to be his wife at his side. In Ezekiel 16 the Lord is pictured as finding an abandoned girl. He rescues her. Later he comes back and wants to marry her. But she is not ready. *'Then I washed you with water'* says

the Lord. It is a picture of the way the Lord Jesus Christ has to cleanse us before we are ready to fully function as his beautiful bride and companion.

Jesus washes his church. The 'water' of Ephesians 5:26 cannot be water-baptism, for three reasons. One: the picture language is known in the Old Testament and water-baptism was not the practice of Old Testament believers. Two: it is referring to something Jesus does to his entire church. I do not think the Lord is ever pictured as water-baptising his entire church. Three: this is something that takes place during the entire history of the church, and water-baptism is never viewed that way. This **water-washing** is **with the word**. Jesus washes his church by sending his word to her. God's word is always purifying in its effect.

What is our response to Jesus' purifying in the life of his bride the church?

6. **On our side it is readiness for companionship**. Jesus purifies his bride that he might be united to her. He is the spotless, pure one. He wants his bride to be as pure as he is. Marriage when it is truly as it ought to be is the highest form of companionship. *'Those who belong to Christ Jesus have crucified the flesh with its passions and desires'* (Galatians 5:24). I do not think this refers to all Christians. It refers to those who have become companions of Jesus. They 'belong' to him in a special way. How did they get to enjoy his companionship? They participated in his cleansing their lives.

If we are to be the bride of Christ we cooperate with our heavenly Lord as he cleanses us. He washes us by the *'washing of water with the Word'* (Ephesians 5:26).

7. **On Jesus' side it includes planning**. Jesus is preparing his bride for her destiny. His destiny for her is that she should be utterly ready to be a companion to him for all eternity. He wants to present the church to himself as his companion for ever.

8. **On our side it is zeal that Jesus' plans for us should be fulfilled**. Surely a bride who is passionately in love with her

husband identifies with him closely in everything. She wants to share his mind, his ambitions, his future, his everything. So if you are part of the 'bride of Christ' one would expect unusual zeal for the heavenly husband. 'The bride' wants to bring everyone to see how marvellous her husband is. The Spirit and the bride say 'Come!' The bride is alongside her husband and says 'Come!' She is wanting to explain to everyone what his heart is. She says to everyone 'Come! My bridegroom is wonderful. Come and meet him. Come! Come!'

She cooperates too in getting ready for her destiny. If Jesus is going to get her to be glorious, she wants to start being glorious immediately. If Jesus wants her without spots or wrinkles or blemishes, she wants to start getting rid of spots and wrinkles and blemishes right away.

9. **On Jesus' side it is provision, care**. Jesus wants to nourish his church and cherish his church.

10. **On our side it is faith**. If Jesus wants to nourish and cherish us we trust him to do so. No situation ever brings us into fear. We refuse to be anxious or grumpy or resentful. We trust our heavenly husband to care for us, to bring us all of the way into our destiny.

Is the 'bride of Christ' the whole of the saved or part of the saved? What of Christians who do not respond to their heavenly husband. I am not absolutely sure that I know, but I know this. The Christian who is not ready will in some way be excluded from the joys and marvels and wonders of the day when Jesus comes to present his bride to himself. The church that Jesus presents to himself **will** be holy and without blemish.

Are you Jesus' bride? Then be responding, submitting. Be getting ready. Be zealous. Be trusting. And you will be presented by Jesus to himself.

Chapter 8

The Temple of God

There is no literal temple-building nowadays, nor do we
need one. If anyone ever builds one it will have no special
significance as the fulfilment of Scripture. In ancient
Israel, God's temple was the place where God put his
name or 'glory'. He said *'I will put my name there'* (1 Kings
3:2; 8:16–20, 29; 9:3).

God's name is his glory, his holy presence radiating out.
Sometimes this glory was only known by faith, but inside
the Holy of Holies, it would have been visible to the naked
eye, except that generally speaking no one could go there.
In the ancient temple of Israel it would kill any person to
see the glory of God directly. When the high-priest went
there once a year, a cloud of incense stopped him from
being able to see the glory of God.

The temple was a foretaste of three things. It foreshadowed Jesus. The body of Jesus was a temple of God
(John 2:21). Also, it foreshadowed the church, the fellowship of believers (1 Corinthians 3:16; Ephesians 2:22;
Hebrews 3:6; 1 Peter 2:5; 2 Corinthians 6:16). Also, individual believers are God's temples. Paul said to the
Corinthians *'Your body is a temple of the Holy Spirit'*
(1 Corinthians 6:19).

The main idea of 'temple' is that it is a *'dwelling place of
God'* (Ephesians 2:22).

1. **The church of Jesus Christ is a temple in which everyone is a priest**. In Israel the temple was not open to everyone. Only priests could go inside the actual building itself. But through Jesus Christ, every Christian is a priest. Every Christian has equal rights of access to his king. *'You are a royal priesthood'* said Peter (1 Peter 2:9). All Christians are being built into a spiritual house, to be a holy priesthood, to offer spiritual sacrifices.

2. **The church of Jesus Christ is approached by means of the blood of sacrifice**. At the doorway of the temple was a great altar. The priest could only come inside the temple by means of having his sins set aside by the blood of one who died for him. So it is with Jesus. There is no access to the true church of Jesus except by means of the blood of Jesus. The temple spoke of approaching God by the blood of the lamb. The church of Jesus Christ is the fellowship of people who have come into God's Kingdom by the blood of Jesus.

3. **The church of Jesus Christ is a place of fellowship**. In the ancient temple there were symbolic tables there with bread on them. Jesus is the bread of life and we feed on him. There were also lampstands there. Jesus is the light of the world and we are enlightened by him. There was also a small altar for burning incense. Jesus is interceding for us and our prayers are inter-linked with his prayers.

4. **The church of Jesus Christ is a holy people**. In Israel, the temple was sacred to God. It was 'holy ground'. If anyone desecrated God's temple he was liable to face God's judgement. Paul similarly says *'you yourselves are God's temple. If anyone destroys God's temple, God will destroy him'* (1 Corinthians 3:16, 17). Anything that damages God's church makes God angry. It is sacred to him. We must be careful what we do with regard to the church of Jesus Christ. God has plans for his glorious church. It is to be the place where his name is revealed. To damage it will arouse his anger.

5. **The church of Jesus needs to cultivate great spiritual unity**. The church of Jesus is not finished yet. The building

is still going up. It is to be a place of great unity. We are to be like bricks and stones *'fitly framed together'*. It is still in progress. We are actually being built into each other. In ancient buildings stones needed to be chiselled into shape to fit the gap where the stone was to go. Every Christian is a *'living stone'*. Our presence is needed in the *'holy temple'*. Something will be missing if we are not playing our part. All preaching-ministries are to focus on this. The various ministries are given *'until we all reach the unity in the faith'* (Ephesians 4:13). In the ancient temples of Israel there were barriers. In Herod's temple there was the 'women's court' and there was a dividing wall that kept gentiles out. There was a special place for lepers, and there were areas where only priests could go. The ancient temples were full of barriers. But in the temple of God, the church of Jesus Christ, there are no barriers inside. Even the veil before the holy of holies is taken down. It is all one giant holy of holies where the presence of God may be experienced. All are priests. There is no dividing wall between men and women, between Jew and gentile, between Judean tribe and Levite tribe. The stones are all to be fitly framed together. Loving unity is to be cultivated all the time. As this happens *'there the Lord commands the blessing'* (see Psalm 133).

6. **The temple-blessing of God's people requires deliberate steps of approach**. I use the phrase 'temple-blessing'. To know fellowship with God is an 'experience'. It is something we are to be conscious of. In the days of ancient Israel the temple had to be 'entered'. *'I will enter his gates with thanksgiving...'*. Then there were stages of further entry. First was the porch. You were coming close to the place where God revealed himself. Then there was the holy place. At that point everything the priest saw spoke to him of fellowship with the living God. Then there was the holy of holies. Only the high priest went there once a year. When he went in there, symbolically he was experiencing the highest degree of fellowship. Actually it was all symbolic. It was possible to go there and

feel nothing at all. And when God's glory was there, a cloud of incense prevented the sight of God's brilliant splendour. But now the *'way into the holiest'* is made open. The highest degree of fellowship with God is available. The holy of holies is (if one may speak symbolically) the inner recesses of heaven. It is the throne-room of God. This is what the church of Jesus is to be, God's temple, the place where God is experienced.

This all needed to be deliberately 'entered'. There were very distinct walls and gates around the temple area. You were either inside or you were not. There was no question of not being sure where you were. But persistence is needed if we are to esperience the Lord in the church in the way that we desire. *'We are God's house'* says Hebrews 3:6) *'if we hold on to our boldness and the hope of which we boast'*. To actually **experience** the presence of God among his people requires faith and persistency. We shall not have the 'temple-experience' of knowing and feeling God among his people if we do not persist in faith. We must stay open to God's voice. We must refuse to harden our heart. We must refuse to draw back in unbelief. If we do not persist in faith we shall miss the blessings of being God's temple.

7. **The church of Jesus Christ looks for the blessing of being honoured by God's presence**. When the temple was being built there came a point where everything in the temple had been built, and Solomon then looked for the glory of God to come down upon what he had done. In 1 Kings 8 Solomon had a sure and certain knowledge that he had done what God would honour. To know that what one is doing is in the will of God brings great faith, and great faith brings great blessing. Day by day, the church is to look for the day when God will honour what is happening by the giving of his glory. What would we think if after all of Solomon's seven years of building God had not come down in glory? The confirmation that Solomon was right to build the temple was that God honoured him by coming down in obvious blessing. The cloud, the divine

nature became partially visible. It came down and filled the temple (1 Kings 8:10–11). This was the greatest proof there could be that Solomon's work was truly in God's will. God honoured everything that Solomon had done.

God honoured Solomon despite his imperfections. He had great weaknesses. There were aspects of his kingship which fell short of what he should have been as an Israelite king. Yet God can use his servants even when they are very far from being perfect. Solomon had made big mistakes in his life, but this did not prevent God from honouring him.

This is what the church of Jesus Christ looks for more than anything else. It looks for the glory of God to come down upon it. We look for the glory of God in the church's worship, in the church's preaching, in the church's mission of mercy to the world. This is what happened in the story of the early church and we expect it to happen again.

Just as Solomon had many weaknesses yet it was God's will that the temple should be built and that God's glory should come down and God's 'name' – the radiation of his character – would be there within the holy of holies. Something similar is to happen in the story of the church. The church is God's temple. It is going up but is not yet finished. We expect the glory of God to come down upon it in the way that the glory of God came down upon the temple that Solomon built. Human weaknesses will not stop God from honouring his church, just as human weaknesses did not stop God from honouring his temple in the days of Solomon.

Chapter 9

The Body of Christ

Another piece of 'picture-language' that is used to describe God's worldwide church is that of 'the body'.

It is a curious fact that when those of us who are preachers or Christian leaders talk about the church as 'the body' we often become rather confused as to whether we are talking about the local church or the universal church or both at the same time. Actually the term 'body' generally refers to the entire company of saved people on earth at any given time.

It is **not** generally referring to all of the saved on earth **and in heaven**. Some have said that Christ's 'body, the church' is a purely heavenly body, a heavenly assembly. But I do not think this is quite right. When, for example, Paul says something like *'I complete what is lacking in Christ's afflictions for the sake of his body, the church, of which I became a minister'* he is surely thinking of people **on earth**. Apparently the church must suffer in order to bring in the final age of Jesus the Messiah. Paul shares a large amount of this suffering for the sake of the church. However the thought implies that 'the church' is an earthly body. A **purely** heavenly body would not be able to suffer.

True, the 'headquarters' of this church is heaven. True, it is an assembly gathered around Jesus who is in heaven, an assembly which has never yet seen itself as one complete assembly, an assembly whose assembling is still in progress. 'The body, the church' certainly has heavenly aspects but I doubt whether it is right to define it as **purely** a heavenly body. The 'body', the church, is rather the entire company of Christians **on earth** who are viewed as assembled with their heavenly Lord. True, they are all 'seated in the heavenly places', but they are very much on earth as well!

Equally, the term 'body' is not **specially** focusing on the local congregation. The term 'body' is always to be seen as a reference to the universal church. It is not that local churches are 'bodies' of Christ. The term 'church' can be used in the plural – 'churches'. But the picture of the body is never used in the plural; we never have reference to the 'bodies' of Christ.

There are characteristics of the universal church, the 'body of Christ' that do not apply to the local church. *'There is one body'*, says Paul (Ephesians 4:4). This cannot be said of the local church. There are **many** churches, in this sense.

It is true that as soon as one talks of the universal church as the 'body of Christ' one finds oneself referring to the local situation. 'The church' is, seen in 'the churches'. Yet Paul's use of 'church' and 'body' has the entire company of believers in mind.

The term 'body' comes in the writings of Paul (Romans 12:4, 5; 1 Corinthians 10:16–17; 12:12–20, 22–25, 27; Ephesians 1:23; 2:16; 4:4, 12, 16; 5:23, 28, 30; Colossians 1:18; 2:19; 3:15 and in Hebrews 13:3). The emphasis varies in different letters. In Romans and 1 Corinthians the main point is that the church is a body with many members. In Ephesians and Colossians the main point is that the church is a body with a head.

1. **'Body' stresses the idea of life**. Think of the difference between a machine and a body. A machine may have motion but it is rigid, routine, programmed, mechanical, mindless. A human person is not a machine. People have flexibility. Their routines may be adapted moment by

moment to the needs of the situation. A person may think about what he is doing. He or she may be unpredictable, may act surprisingly.

The supreme characteristic of the church is its life, or (as I prefer to put it) its liveliness. The church of Jesus may be organised, but that is not the most important thing about it. The main characteristic of the church of Jesus is that the source of the church's life is God Himself.

2. **'Body' stresses the source of life**. The liveliness flows from the Head into the body. This may not be biologically scientific but it is the way Paul is using his illustration. The people of God are alive 'in Christ'. Spiritual life or liveliness comes by being joined on to Jesus. Men and women make machines, but God imparts life. Nothing in God's creation, that has any life in it, is robotic or machine-like. So it is with the church, the body of Christ. God-imparted life is the essence of the church. Only God can add to this church. When someone is converted to Jesus, the Spirit of God places that person into the body of Christ (1 Corinthians 12:13). He or she is part of a living organism, alive with the life of God, fulfilling its calling by being daily empowered by God.

The source of this life is Jesus. He gives energy; he gives the desire for worship. He gives the ability to put down sin and work out our salvation in godly living. He gives the true members of the true church love and concern for each other. All this is the liveliness flowing from Jesus, the head of the church, into his body. In writing to the Colossians Paul makes the point that the church does not need any **other** source of life besides Jesus. He refers to heresies and false teaching that depend on philosophy and tradition (Colossians 2:8) and legalism (Colossians 2:16). Then he says (Colossians 2:18, 19) *'You do not need any of these things. Let no one condemn you, delighting in slavish lowliness and worship of angels, which he has seen while 'entering' into religious experience. Such a person is puffed up by his unspiritual mind and he or she is not holding to the Head, from which the whole body, nourished and held together* *through the joints and ligaments, grows with a growth that is from God.'*

This is the point of the 'body' language. The entire church of Jesus Christ has nourishment from the Head, from Jesus himself.

3. **'Body' language stresses unity**. Think of the tight unity that exists in the human body. An arm cannot be separated from the body without bad mutilation or amputation. There are very deep ties between the parts of a human body. So it is with the church of Jesus Christ (1 Corinthians 12:4, 5, 6, 12–13; 10:17; Ephesians 4:4–6). It has a **given** unity, a deep unity, a unity that includes unity of mind. In this 'one body', there is 'one faith' (Ephesians 4:4, 5). There is fellow-feeling and sympathy. *'Remember those who are in chains'* said the letter to the Hebrews, *'as people who are bound with them ... as people who are themselves also in the body'* (Hebrews 13:3). The body of Christ may have within it those who have traditionally been enemies but God brings them together. Jews and gentiles hated each other in the first century but Jesus *'made the two groups into one'* and created *'in himself out of the two groups, one new humanity, making peace'*, reconciling *'the two in one body, for God, through the cross'* (Ephesians 2:16; see also Ephesians 3:5, 6; Colossians 3:15).

4. **'Body' language stresses variety**. Not only is there amazing unity in a body, there is also amazing variety. There is one body but *'many parts to it'* (1 Corinthians 12:14). This is the way it is in the Christian church. One part is doing one aspect of the work of God. Another part is doing another aspect of the work of God. This is true not only within the local congregation. It is also true at a worldwide level. The church of Jesus Christ holds to *'one faith'* in Jesus everywhere, but different parts of the world are strong at different points. The churches of Korea can teach us something of prayer. The churches in China can teach about evangelism in the midst of persecution. Some of the revived churches of Africa can teach us much about

dedication and zeal. Some of the churches of the West are strong in their grasp of Scripture. The churches of Latin America are strong in their ability to sweep aside centuries of traditionalism. We have many parts in the same body and all the parts do not have the same ministry (Romans 12:4, 5).

5. **'Body' language tells us that we are related to each other, and are to help each other**. We are all related to Christ. I am joined on to my fellow Christian as my hand is on to my arm. There is within a body a unity of life, of blood-circulation, of nervous energy, of ligaments. There is a deep organic unity.

6. **'Body' language implies that we should yield ourselves to serve the entire Christian fellowship everywhere**. Otherwise the whole body will suffer. Romans 12:4-5 tells us that we are one body in Christ, and then says *'Having gifts that differ let us use them'* (Romans 12:6). This is **how** we yield our bodies and are *'transformed in the renewing of our minds'* (Romans 12:1–2). We yield ourselves to his people. We aim to be a blessing to other Christians.

7. **'Body' language speaks of the growth of the body**. Living out the truth in love we are to grow in Jesus in all things. Jesus is the Head and we grow *'in him who is the head'* (Ephesians 4:15–16). It is *'from him'*, the head of the body, that *'the whole body fitted together and knitted together through every connecting point and every provision, according to the working in measure of each one part ... makes the growth of the body for the upbuilding of itself in love'*.

8. **'Body' language speaks of the Lordship of Jesus Christ**. He is the head, the king, the leader, the guide, the source of energy. Everything comes from him. Everything he does returns to give him glory.

Chapter 10

The Holy Nation

Another way the church is pictured is as a *'holy nation'*. *'You people are a chosen generation, a royal priesthood, a holy nation, a people for God's own possession'* says the apostle Peter (1 Peter 2:9, 10). All of this is language taken from the nation of Israel. 1 Peter, more than any other part of the New Testament, takes phrases that originally applied to the nation of Israel and applies them to the church. 1 Peter 2:9, 10 take descriptions of Israel from Exodus 19:6, Isaiah 43:20–21 and Hosea chapters 1 and 2, and it applies those descriptions to the Christians that Peter is writing to. They are mainly gentiles although some of them may have been Jews.

Israel is a picture of the church. I have written above that 'the church' is the nation of Israel reduced to a remnant and having gentiles grafted into it. So 'the church' is the form in which spiritual 'Israel' exists. There is an earthly nation of Israel **also**, but God's saved 'Israel' is the church. The nation of Israel is a 'picture', a 'type', of the church. The church is God's holy nation just as the nation of Israel was God's holy nation. A change came during the ministry of Jesus. *'The kingdom of God shall be taken away from you'*, said Jesus to the leaders of Israel, *'and shall be given to a nation bringing forth its fruits'* (Matthew 21:43). The church is the new nation to which God's kingly rule is given. Ephesians chapter 2 makes the same point. The gentile Ephesians were no longer *'gentiles in the flesh'* (Ephesians 2:11), no longer alienated from the citizenship of Israel (Ephesians 2:12). Since they had come to know Jesus they were *'fellow citizens with the saints'* (Ephesians 2:19). They had a new citizenship, in a new holy nation, in the worldwide church of Jesus Christ with both Jews and gentiles in it.

Let us follow what this means by looking at Peter's four phrases. *'You people are a chosen generation, a royal priesthood, a holy nation, a people for God's own possession'* (1 Peter 2:9, 10).

1. **The church of Jesus is a 'chosen generation'**. The word 'generation' is rather difficult to translate. It means 'offspring', 'progeny', a nation of descendants from a common father, a clan.

Think of the way in which we can recognise people that come from the same clan or family or section of the human race. Certain nationalities have a particular skin colour. Or they may be characteristically tall or characteristically short. They may tend to have brown eyes, as do certain nationalities in the human family. We are able to recognise a particular 'race' or sub-section of humankind.

This is the idea behind what Peter writes. *'You are a chosen offspring, a chosen sub-section of the human race.'* The main idea is that the church of Jesus is recognisable because its members all have a common parenthood. They are like a clan which all descend from a single ancestor. The point is that God is the Father of all Christians and that their 'descent' from a common father is recognisable. *'Be ye imitators of God, as beloved children'*, said Paul (Ephesians 5:1). The reason why we are able to be like God is that we are his beloved children. This is what the church, of Jesus Christ is. It is a chosen generation, a chosen 'race', a group of people who all show family resemblance to their heavenly Father.

What is it that makes us a 'race' like this? It is because we were 'chosen'. You are a **'chosen** generation' says Peter. I do not understand this biblical teaching that we are 'chosen' by God. But although I do not understand it I believe it. I do not know why God chose me; I only know that did because he worked in me faith in Jesus. *'Those who were ordained for eternal life believed'* (Acts 13:48). I do not understand it, but I believe it. This is what the church is, the company of those who because they were chosen by God have become God's new holy race, a holy people, all having God as their Father. We are a people who all have the same Father, a people who are brothers and sisters, a people who are conscious that we have a heavenly Father that others do not have.

2. **The church of Jesus is a 'royal priesthood'.** Once again the idea is taken from the descriptions of Israel. The nation of Israel was intended to be a nation of kings and priests, a 'royal family' (as the word might be translated) and a 'priesthood'. In ancient Israel there was a sense in which **every** Israelite was meant to be a priest. It is true that there was one tribe of priests, the descendants of Aaron who formed the tribe of Levi. Yet it was also true that in a sense every Israelite was meant to be a priest. The whole nation were meant to be priests to God. The nation was to be a nation of priests.

It is this phrase (taken by Peter from Exodus 19:6) that is to be applied to the church of Jesus. The entire church of Jesus is a nation of royal priests.

What does it mean to be a priest? A priest is a person who has access to God. In Israel priests could go inside the tabernacle or inside the temple. They had access to the presence of God. The church of Jesus is a nation in which every citizen has access to God. Other members of the human race do not have the kind of access to God that the Christians have.

A priest offers sacrifice. Every Christian offers sacrifices to God, sacrifices of worship, the sacrifice of his or her own body, the acts of sacrifice that consists of what we do for God. We are all priests offering ourselves and our praises up to God.

A priest is a person who intercedes. The priest stood

before God on behalf of others and offered up a sacrifice for another. He also prayed for that other person. Every Christian is to be an intercessor. The Christian church is a company of people who know what it is to stand before God presenting requests and prayers for others. We are a kingdom of priests.

We are a 'royal house' as well as priests. In Israel priests were from the tribe of Levi and kings were to come from the tribe of Judah. So you could not be a king and a priest at the same time. But the Christian church is *'a royal priesthood'* or *'a royal family and a priesthood'*. It means that we both reign in Christ as kings, and we intercede before God as priests.

3. **The church of Jesus is a 'holy nation'**. A nation might have a king. The nation of Israel was at one time a nation of people under a God-appointed king. This is what the church of Jesus is, a holy nation under Jesus the king. Each member of the Christian church is ruled by Jesus and shows allegiance to Jesus.

A nation often has a distinctive language. So the Christian church has a distinctive language. It has its own vocabulary. It loves to talk about 'the blood of Christ' and 'faith' and being 'saved' and 'growing in grace'. It is all part of the church's holy language.

A nation has its own customs. So the church of Jesus has customs and traditions. It is a 'holy nation'. We are a people who pray, a people who love God, a people who look for the power of the Holy Spirit. These are our holy customs because we are a holy nation. Many nations of the world are easily recognisable because the citizens of that country have a certain national character. The character of our spiritual country is holiness. It is a holy nation.

The members of a nation are ambassadors for their country. People get a certain impression of their country because of what the citizens of that country are like. The Christian is a member of a 'holy nation'. He has a heavenly citizenship, a heavenly allegiance. Others get an impression of what the 'holy nation' is like as they look at the members of the nation, the individual Christian.

4. **The church of Jesus is 'a people for God's own posses-sion'**. Of all of the expressions in 1 Peter 2 this is the nicest. What is the difference between these different words, a kingdom, a nation, a race, a people. They are all similar words and yet they emphasise slightly different things. It is the word that emphasises God's affection for us. He sees us as his own people, as the people he specially loves. John the Baptist came *'to prepare a people who shall be fit for the Lord'* (Luke 1:17). James once said that from the gentiles God *'chose from among them a people to bear his name'* (Acts 15:14).

God wants to bring into being a community of people who will be specially his. He steps into their lives and brings them to himself. He is taking for himself a people. He has great affection for them. He looks upon them with love. They are his people. He specially owns them and cares for them in a way that is the privilege of no others on planet earth.

The opposite of being 'a people', according to Hosea, is to be *'not a people'*. Once all of us Christians were *'not a people'*. We were not special to God in our experience. We were not experiencing his mercy. We were not reflecting his love. We were not being specially blessed by him. We had no sense of identity that was worth having. But now we are a people! The Christian church is the company of individuals who have been taken by God out of the world and made to be 'a people'. We have a sense of belonging to one another.

Peter goes on in 1 Peter 2:9 to tell us what this holy 'nationality' is intended to do in our lives. It is all so that we might belong to God and radiate for him. It is *'so that you may show forth the excellence of him who called you out of darkness into his marvellous light'*.

What a sense of **privilege** it ought to give us to belong to this holy nation. We all know of nationalities or tribes that are so proud of their nationality. But what a privilege to be in this 'holy nation'. Every one of us in this nation is part of the royal family!

What a sense of **togetherness** it ought to work into our lives. When you are abroad and you meet someone of your own nationality you immediately tend to be warm towards that other person. He is your fellow countryman! All over the world every Christian is our fellow-citizen in the kingdom of God.

What a sense of **responsibility** it should bring to us. We are representing our king! We make claims as God's holy people so the world looks at us to see what it means to have been rescued from our sins.

PART THREE

Ministry in the Church

Chapter 11

The Head of the Church

A major matter of importance in the universal church is ministry. The church of Jesus Christ is meant to minister, to serve, to be like Jesus who came not to be ministered unto but to minister (Mark 10:45).

Ministry begins with Jesus. He is the head of the church. Then ministry flows through the teaching gifts that Jesus gives to his church. Then the various kinds of teaching ministers train every member of the church of Jesus Christ for ministry. That is at least the theory, and increasingly it is to be the reality as the church of Jesus grows in maturity.

Jesus is the 'head' of the church. He is the leader. It is important to grasp hold of this concept on a large scale. It is not simply that Jesus is leading little congregations, although that in itself is true. But, more important, Jesus is leading his people through the course of the history of the church.

1. **In the early days of the church, Jesus led his church through days of persecution**. It would be over-simple to divide up church history as though it fitted into periods with each period having only one characteristic. Yet there are clear differences in the different centuries through which Jesus has led his people. From the day of Pentecost until about the year 312 AD, the Roman empire was hostile to the church and Jesus led his people through

days of persecution. At that time many Christians were executed or thrown to the lions in the Roman arenas. But the Christians were famous for their love and their purity and the church grew despite persecution. In AD 312 the Roman emperor Constantine professed conversion and made 'Christianity' the state religion. Persecution has often come since those days, but Jesus has shown he can lead his people through persecution.

2. **From about AD 312 to about AD 1517 Jesus led his people despite despite days of traditionalism and deadness**. Becoming a 'state-religion' under Constantine did not help the gospel. The professing church at that time slowly was corrupted and eventually became dead and full of false traditions. Mary was worshipped. Salvation was thought to be by infant-baptism. The church became 'the catholic church'. Truly born-again Christians were rare. The Bible was lost to the people, because few could read Greek or Latin. The popes were corrupt. The monasteries tried to bring reform but eventually they also became corrupt. One might think the church ceased to exist! But no! The gates of hell do not prevail against Jesus' church. Jesus had his people throughout those dark days. Sometimes they struggled to maintain spiritual reality within the deadness of the nominal church. Sometimes they became an underground movement. We scarcely know much about the liveliest Christians of those days. They were 'underground' and became a remnant working for better days. But Jesus was with them. He was still the head of his church.

3. **From about AD 1517 to the end of the 18th century, a great reform and revival took place**. First there were men like Martin Luther and John Calvin and others who went back to the Bible and urged that the professing church should be reformed according to the Word of God. They went back to the Bible in a new way. Salvation by faith in Jesus was rediscovered in Europe. After the Reformation of the sixteenth century, groups broke away from being state-churches. Believers' baptism began to be practised in

some circles. Translations of the Bible were made into the ordinary languages of Europe. There was a great movement of the Spirit which began in the 1730s.

The point is: in all of this Jesus was leading his church. He was taking it somewhere and he knew where he was going.

4. **From about the 1790s onwards it was an age of expansion.** From the 1790s the church began to expand into all of the world. India and Africa and South America were reached with the gospel. The gospel went into all the world as never before. Jesus was leading his church into every corner of the globe.

5. When was the end of that phase of the church which I dated as beginning in about the 1790s? It is difficult to say. Recent history is more difficult to see sweepingly than older history. But I would suggest some great changes came in the 1960s. What age are we in now? It seems that we are now in **a day of restoration**. There is new emphasis on the Holy Spirit, on the powers of the Spirit, on revival, on five-fold ministry. Many things forgotten about are coming back into the church of Jesus Christ. What is to happen in the future? Who knows? One thing is sure. Jesus is still the head of his church. He is not going to turn back into previous centuries. The precise characteristics of previous centuries have gone. We shall never be in precisely the days of Luther and Calvin again. The missionary movement of the nineteenth century is finished and in its old form (heavily dependent on the colonial movement and Western imperialism), it must be allowed to fall aside. God's way of reaching the nations is likely to be totally new. Westerners who use 19th century methods of being 'missionaries' are incredibly out of touch and often are racist (and get cheated out of their money very speedily!)

The point is that Jesus is leading the church still. He is its head. Our task is not to follow ancient methods but to see what he is doing in this world and do it with him.

How does he lead his church? Ephesians 4 tells us that

he ascended to the right hand of the Father. From his glorious position as head and king of the church he poured out gifts upon his church. Ephesians 4:11 does not refer to 'spiritual gifts' which people have. Rather it refers to different kinds of people that God gives to his church. The **person** is the gift.

Jesus *'gave some as apostles, some as prophets, some as evangelists, some as pastors and teachers'* (Ephesians 4:11). The purpose of these people who are given to the church is *'for the equipping of the holy people unto the work of ministry, unto the upbuilding of the body of Christ'*. The five-fold ministry of five kinds of Christian preacher are given to the church to equip the church for ministry. The whole church ministers. Certain kinds of preachers and lesders are the trainers that train the whole church to minister.

There is a goal in view. This headship of Jesus over his church, and this pouring of gifts upon his church continues *'until we all reach to the unity of faith and the unity of knowing the Son of God, until we reach to being the complete man, until we reach to the measure of the stature of the fullness of Christ'* (Ephesians 4:13). This is to last for the whole of church history until Jesus comes again. There is a goal in sight. *'All of this is in order that we might no longer be babies, tossed and carried around by every wind of teaching, in the cunning of people, in craftiness, by wiles of deceit'* (Ephesians 4:14). There is a deeper unity among Christians that is coming, deeper than anything that has ever been known before. *'Practising the truth in love we are to grow into him in all things, in him who is the Head, Christ, from whom the whole body fitted together and knitted together through every connecting point and every provision produces ... the growth of the body for the upbuilding of itself in love'* (Ephesians 4:15, 16). This is what is involved in the Headship of our Lord Jesus Christ. He is leading his church into a glorious future. Our task is to see what he is doing in our age and do it with him.

Chapter 12

Apostles

I changed my mind about apostleship about eleven years ago. Like many Bible-believing Christians I had been taught that apostles were a one-generation affair, that apostles had to be eye-witnesses of the resurrection, that they had to be commissioned by the literal, physical and bodily-present Lord Jesus Christ and that by definition no one today could be an apostle. They were the unique one-generation-only foundation of the church. Their work was to lay down the infallible teaching upon which the church was built, and to write – in conjunction with a few other non-apostolic figures – the New Testament. Only certain extremist Pentecostals and peculiar groups like the Mormons and the Irvingites taught that apostles continued in the churches.

All of that I was taught and taught myself until about eleven years ago.

But then I changed my mind.

What made me change my mind? It was the Bible. I happened to meet Harry Das, a man I had known of for some years but had never, until that time, met personally. He had what was called an 'apostolic' ministry. I had never given much thought to the matter before but he put it to me that in Ephesians 4:11 it is the ascended Lord Jesus Christ who gives apostles to his church, and therefore the apostles being referred to are a **post-ascension** matter, and that there was therefore a giving of apostles to the church that was subsequent to the ascension of Jesus. It could not refer to the twelve apostles or to any giving of apostles before the ascension. I was surprised. I had never seen that before and it certainly made me look at things in a new light. Although I had never had any connections with anything that used the term 'apostle' in this way, I almost immediately felt that what he was saying was right and that I would have to reconsider the matter.

Today I hold a different conviction from the one I grew up with as a young Christian. I still believe there is a lot of truth in the old way of putting things and that the first generation of apostles was unique – but there is more that needs to be said.

In the rest of this chapter I want to do three things: (i) to put as compactly as I can the case for modern apostles; (ii) to make some qualifications and disclaimers; and (iii) to make a few comments on the practicalities of the matter.

Firstly, **I think the Bible certainly teaches continuing apostleship**. It must be realised that there are several different types of apostle. There are at least six of them. (i) There is Jesus who is a unique apostle (Hebrews 3:1). (ii) There are the twelve. (iii) Then there are other apostles that I would call 'eye-witness apostles'. They were apostles **and** they had literally seen the risen Jesus. This does not mean though that being an eye-witness is crucial to the definition of every kind of apostle. In 1 Corinthians 9:1 (*'Am I not an apostle? Have I not seen Jesus Christ...?'*) Paul is making two points, not one point. It is not: Am I not an apostle by virtue of the fact that I have seen Jesus? It is rather: Am I not an apostle? And furthermore have I not also seen Jesus...? (iv) There were post-ascension apostles. After his ascension Jesus gave gifts to his church. Among his gifts were apostles. There is no reason to think that there is any reference to the Twelve. Nor do these apostles have to have been eye-witnesses of the resurrection. (v) There are what two verses call the

73

'apostles of the churches'. The key term here is 'of churches'. They were not commissioned delegates of Jesus; they were commissioned delegates of churches. Modern translations rightly use the word 'messengers', but it needs to be borne in mind that the Greek word is the same – apostles. (vi) Then of course the New Testament refers to false apostles.

It is the fourth of the categories that concerns us. Ephesians 4:11 clearly portrays something that is dependent on and subsequent to Jesus' resurrection. And Ephesians 4:11 clearly says that these five-fold teaching gifts continue 'until we all attain' to the glorious description of the church mentioned in Ephesians 4:13–16. It is surely obvious that the description of the church in Ephesians 4:13–16 was not reached in one generation. Yet Ephesians 4 seems to say that the five-fold teaching gifts continue until such a time is reached. The whole argument seems positively to imply that apostles continue.

In the story of the church, biblical concepts have often been dismissed as 'for the New Testament age only'. One subject after another has had to be restored to the church. One must remember that Matthew 28:19–20 was once assumed to be a one-generation affair until William Carey forcefully pointed out that the phrase 'to the close of the age' implies that the command also continues to the end of the age.

It is also like 1 Corinthians 13:8 (*'as for prophecy, it will pass away; as for tongues, they will cease'*). Again it was argued for centuries that these matters were a one-generation affair. But again the surrounding context (1 Corinthians 13:10) seems to imply that the **timing** of the cessation is the second coming of Jesus.

Anyone who thinks that Matthew 28:18–20 lasts to the end of the age ought also to think that the gifts of 1 Corinthians 12–14 must continue to the end of the age. But by the same argumentation such a one will be led on to conclude that apostleship lasts to the end of the age also.

Certainly as I considered the matter some years ago, it seemed peculiar to me that men and women in denominational structures with general assemblies and synods and boards and travelling secretaries and general secretaries and committees and scores of sub-sections and committees should complain that apostles were unscriptural! 'Surely', I said to myself, 'it is better to have some kind of structure that resembles the way things were done in the New Testament rather than structures that do not resemble anything in the New Testament.' Surely to have circles of apostolic ministry resembles the New Testament more than the structures I saw and worked with in the early days of my Christian life. Since that time I have come to have some experience of how apostleship works in practice and am now doubly and trebly convinced that apostleship works. Apostleship is more practical than the kind of structures that are found in circles that do not have apostles. Which is more biblical? The general assembly? The house of clergy and the house of laity? The annual XYZ Conference? Or circles of apostolic ministry? What possible objection can there be to continuing a pattern which seems to have at least some precedent in the New Testament? Is a Spirit-given vision for God's work likely to come to a hierarchy? I suppose it can, but it seems more often to come to a leadership-team or to a Spirit-filled man who bears a remarkable resemblance to the apostles of the New Testament times.

But secondly **I must make some qualifications and disclaimers**. Modern apostles are type-4 of the ones mentioned above, not type-3. Modern apostles are not writers of Scripture; they do not generate new doctrines. They are not literal eye-witnesses of the resurrection. It used to be said that apostles were the one-generation foundation of the church. It would be better to say that the **first** generation of apostles laid down the definitive pattern for the church and modern apostles cannot depart from the teaching of the **first** generation of apostles. But this does not mean that there cannot be a second generation and a third generation of apostles who also lay the foundations of churches in their days. Such subsequent generations however have to abide by the pattern of doctrine and life laid down by the first generation. We cannot progress beyond New Testament doctrine. All of the concerns of the old evangelical orthodoxy are preserved. No one needs to fear that the idea of modern apostles means new doctrines or anything like that.

The thing is more important than the name. There can be apostles when the word is not being used. And a person can claim to be an apostle when he is no such thing. What is important is the reality, not the word. Hudson Taylor was surely the 'apostle of China' as he is often said to be even by people who do not believe in apostles! But I do not know that he ever claimed to be an apostle. I rather doubt whether he believed there could be apostles. But he surely was one.

It needs to be remembered that every apostle is different in character from every other apostle. Nowadays, when apostleship is being discussed, it seems that we are often looking for the prototype apostle. Must he do this? Or must he do that? Well, there is certainly a basic 'job-description' for an apostle. He has a wide range of spiritual gifts. He is called by God, not by any committee or organisation. He 'manifests' his calling by the ability to do what the first generation of apostles did. He is able to lay down the foundations of church and to bring into being ministries.

But having said this I am wary of more precise descriptions. I know men whose apostolic credentials I would not dispute yet who are very different from each other. Some are large men physically with powerful voices, with the ability to hold together teams of ministry that span continents. Others are ordinary-looking folk with a chatty way of speaking. Yet they have an iron fist inside a velvet glove and are capable of generating and leading enthusiasm for worldwide outreach. The 'kernel' of the idea of an apostle (commission by Jesus, proven ability in spawning churches and ministries, combination of a wide range of gifts) does not mean that they all have to be the same like a row of postage stamps. I know of a number of men who I would say are 'apostles' but no two of them are alike.

Thirdly, **I am concerned about how apostleship works in practice**. It seems to me that only the most gifted men are capable of handling what I would call long-distance apostleship. It is not very easy to live in (say) Australia and oversee churches in (say) mainland China. I am not saying it cannot be done; I am saying that only the most gifted are capable of it. In practice long-distance apostleship requires gifted men. As the work gets bigger the long-distance apostle has to major more and more on matters of structure. Because the numbers are now getting bigger he has greater difficulties in getting his will done with an ever-increasing number. This means when he does visit from a long distance away he has to give his attention to structure as well as to preaching about holiness and the glories of the gospel. Also when disputes arise, there is a danger of his getting to hear of those disputes not through the local people but through one or two leaders only. If he is not careful those who have his ear influence him more than the Holy Spirit influences him. In practice it is important that spiritual people have access to the apostle. He is such a long way away and when he visits his time is short and he has to give his attention to structural matters and matters of controversy that have arisen since his last visit. None of this means that apostleship is wrong. Paul had all of these difficulties and did not have the use of telephone or fax! Yet he laid down the foundations of the churches of the Mediterranean areas in the mid-first century. It simply means that care must be taken in recognising such a large-scale gifting. Such men must have large measures of good judgement and spiritual discernment. Not anyone should be lightly proclaimed to be an apostle.

Certainly the church of Jesus Christ needs apostles, and (whether the word was used or not) has always had them. The church of Jesus Christ needs all five of the preaching ministries of Ephesians 4:11 if it is to get beyond infancy and instability. The whole spread of differing preaching-and-leading gifts will be needed to bring the church to unity in the faith and to the full knowledge of the Son of God. We need apostles, and it would help if we give them their right name.

Chapter 13

Prophets and Evangelists

In recent years the idea of 'five-fold ministry' has been given a lot of attention. The attempts that have been made to follow Ephesians 4:11 have however been very varied in their results. There has been much more willingness in recent years to consider the possibility of the church having 'prophets' than there has been to accept the idea of apostles. Yet I have the feeling that even in charismatic churches the gift of prophecy, as it has been used in the churches, is in need of some reconsideration.

What is 'prophecy'? I would define it as **'speaking for God with words given by God'**. The prophet of the Old Testament was a person into whose mouth God put words (Deuteronomy 18:18; Jeremiah 1:9). To a lesser or greater degree that remains the central definition of prophecy.

1. **It needs to be said that the idea that prophets are only for the apostolic age is difficult to defend**. Without going into long arguments I am taking it for granted that there can be prophets today. I have not always believed that. I used to be taught that prophecy and prophets were not for today. Then I came to feel that the gift of prophecy could continue but that there could not be prophets. Then eventually I came to think that there is no biblical reason why there cannot be prophets today. Ephesians 4:11 clearly portrays them as part of God's five-fold gift to the church and gives no hint that these gifts are only a temporary

matter. They continue until the church reaches final maturity.

2. **There are changes when one moves from Old Testament prophecy to New Testament prophecy**. Old Testament prophets were obviously very special people. The Old Testament prophet had to have a special call from God. He had a special awareness of what God was doing in history. He spoke to his own day but was sometimes given to know about events that were yet to happen. His messages did not **have** to be predictive, however. These prophets continued all the way until the last one, who was John the Baptist (Matthew 11:13). These prophets were **people who spoke for God with words given by God**.

There are differences between an Old Testament prophet and a New Testament prophet. In the days of the Old Testament the prophet was the supreme preaching ministry in Israel. Only Moses was greater. In the days of the New Covenant that position is occupied by apostles and prophets are second to the apostles.

3. **The gift of prophecy is the greatest of the gifts of the Spirit**. We are told to *'earnestly desire the spiritual gifts but especially that we may prophesy'* (1 Corinthians 14:1). This is important in interpreting the gift of prophecy. Some things that today are called 'prophecy' could hardly be regarded as the greatest of all the spiritual gifts.

4. **The 'prophet' is a person who is regularly and frequently used by God with the gift of prophecy**. One can prophesy without being a prophet. Not everyone who is occasionally given what he should say by God is a 'prophet'.

In New Testament times, as well as the gift of prophecy being found in many Christians, there were also certain men and women who were frequently used by God in this way and they were recognised as prophets. So there were New Testament prophets as well as Old Testament prophets. A modern 'prophet' is simply one who is used by God with the gift of prophecy in a regular and frequent way, such that it is his main ministry.

5. **We must grasp what a modern prophet cannot do**. He cannot write a new Bible or add to the Bible we already have. He cannot put forward new doctrines. He cannot give us information about biblical teaching that is more detailed than the biblical teaching itself. I recall hearing a man once who gave teaching about what goes on in hell. He claimed he had been to hell; his descriptions concerning the activities of hell were more detailed than any teaching we have on that subject in the Bible. Such men should be ignored. Any teaching that gives a doctrine beyond the teaching of the New Testament is to be rejected.

6. **There are certain areas where a modern prophet must be specially careful**. The modern prophet must be careful about talking as if he were God. He must be careful about directive prophecies. He must be careful about predictive prophecies concerning modern political events. I do not say God can never give a word concerning such matters. I have given prophecies concerning international political events myself. I simply say that great care is needed.

7. **We must consider what one expects true prophecy to be like**. I am not very impressed by what some people call 'prophecy' in many modern churches. Someone stands up and says something like 'The Lord is with you. My children, be ready to take this nation for God. I am about to give you many blessings, only you must be obedient to me . . .', and so on. I agree with every word of it, but I am not sure it is prophecy! I can hardly think that **that** was what Paul had in mind when he spoke of prophecy as the gift to be sought above all others. The gift of prophecy is a kind of preaching although it is not textual preaching or Bible exposition. It is where the speaker, man or woman, is aware that he or she is being specially guided in what to say and – although the person's mind is working normally – one can sense that God is giving what should be said. It is powerfully convincing. It is strongly directive. Although not as authoritative as the work of an apostle it is the greatest gift in the life of the church.

8. **Prophecies should be tested**. When someone claims to be giving a word from God, they are sometimes immediately recognisable as coming from God. Sometimes the leader should say 'We must consider whether this is a word from God' and give leaders time to consider what has been said. Sometimes it may take days for the word to be thoroughly weighed. The New Testament says that in a fellowship meeting people may prophesy but he adds *'let others discern'* (1 Corinthians 14:29). Other people with similar gifts of teaching and revelation were to judge the prophesying. The teaching had to be in harmony with the first generation of apostolic teaching. In Old Testament times the prophet's teaching had to be in harmony with the revelation given through Moses. False prophets are self-appointed, and are play-acting. The prophet's message does not have to be **narrowly** personal. It may cover some aspect of what the church needs to hear concerning sin and judgement, grace and salvation.

Another gift to the church is the evangelist. The word means 'preacher of good news'. The evangelist is a man or woman whose task it is to focus on the central message of salvation. There is a difference between *'the whole counsel of God'* (as Paul put it to the elders of Ephesus in Acts 20:17, 27), and the narrower message of *'repentance and faith'* (which Paul says he preached to unconverted Jews and Greeks (Acts 20:21)). If one considers the evangelistic sermons of the book of Acts and then considers (for example) the themes of Romans or Ephesians, one discovers a much narrower message in the 'evangelistic' message. Some themes of Paul's letters get no mention in Paul's evangelistic messages to the unsaved. The 'evangelist' is not a teacher of the whole counsel of God. He takes the central themes concerning sin and salvation, Christ and his cross, repentance and faith, and he presses the need of faith upon the unconverted. Some people are specially given to the church who are specifically used by God in this way. They are the church's 'evangelists'. They should not be 'free-lance' preachers but should be closely linked to the churches and to apostolic leadership.

Such apostles and prophets and evangelists are not produced by universities or by committees. They are given directly to the church by God. They 'manifest' themselves. They emerge as the church's life goes forward. They have a calling from God and slowly move forward into the ministries that God has given them. They take time to be trained by God himself. The greater the ministry the richer the experience that God gives to the person concerned. The greater the ministry the longer it will take the person concerned to get there. Apostles do not become apostles overnight. Even Paul had ten hidden years of his life before he suddenly started becoming famous in Antioch.

Exactly how they emerge is up to God. The church's task is not to create apostles or prophets or evangelists but to recognise them when God gives them and give opportunities for their particular giftedness to be used.

These gifts are gifts to the **whole** church, not simply to local congregations. Prophets and evangelists do not stay locked within one congregation. They work closely with apostles and with circles of churches which God has brought together.

Chapter 14

Pastors and Teachers

Two more of the five-fold ministries are the pastors and teachers. The Greek wording of Ephesians 4:11 is put in such a way that it ties the words together, 'pastors-and-teachers'. Some have thought that this means there are four gifts to the church, apostles, prophets, evangelists and a fourth group who are pastors-and-teachers. But there can be no doubt that there are some men who are more pastors than teachers and other men who are more teachers than pastors.

I use the word 'men'. Generally these positions will be occupied by men. The question might be raised and may be answered here briefly: Where do women fit into all of this? May there be women apostles, women prophets, women evangelists, women pastors, women teachers? A few sentences cannot do justice to the subject. All I can say is that there seem to be plenty of indications in the Bible that women may do almost everything that men do. There are abundant references to women travelling in ministry, assisting Jesus, prophesying, praying and doing certain kinds of teaching. There seems to be only **one** area that is not given to women and that is being the final authority in the matter of teaching. This seems to be the point of 1 Timothy 2. Even so I do not think it forbids a woman teaching in a way that is **not** claiming to be the supreme authority in any given situation. 'Women's ministry' seems to be a very Western preoccupation. In most of the world women minister a great deal in pulpits and out of them, but this does not mean that they have supreme authority in leadership. In situations of revival women are used much by God as well as men, but they stay within the limits laid down by 1 Timothy 2. Men and women are different and on the whole men are to be the leaders within the church. Women may minister a great deal so long as they bear this proviso in mind.

The **pastors** are the shepherds. They are linked with the teachers because they do their shepherding by the teaching of God's Word. The different kinds of preaching-minister give their time to different things. The apostle is the person with a wide range of gifts, a person capable of superintending and pioneering new ministries. He spends much time in administering the churches. The prophet is not much of an adminiatrator. He gives more time than most to prayer and fellowship with God. The evangelist spends a lot of time travelling. The teacher spends a lot of time with his Bible. The pastor spends a lot of time with **people**. He is a shepherd of people. He counsels them, guides them, prays with them and for them. They are like the 'shepherds' of Ezekiel 34 – which actually refers to Israelite kings. There is a connection in the Bible between kingship and shepherding. The kings of Israel were shepherds. The model king, David, was a shepherd as well as a king. His skill at shepherding sheep was retained when he began as king to shepherd people.

The king-shepherds of Ezekiel 34:1–18 are people who strengthen the weak (Ezekiel 34:4), heal the sick, bind up the injured, and bring back the lost. The 'pastor' has gifts in this direction. He is unusually gifted in care and concern.

The **teachers** give themselves to the teaching of the entire Christian faith. They are not apostles, since they do not have gifts of large-scale superintendence. They do not give themselves readily to committees and administration. They are not evangelists since their giftedness covers a wider range of topics. They are not as gifted as the 'pastor' with people, although the teacher has to be a bit of a pastor as well. He is not a university lecturer! His teaching is for ordinary people. He is a 'shepherd' but he – more than others – does his shepherding by the direct teaching of God's Word.

The teacher gives himself to steady regular careful public teaching of a largish body of material. In the gospels we find Jesus 'teaching' publicly in the synagogue, in the temple courts, in the open air. Luke chapter 4 is one of the fullest descriptions of what this involved in the synagogue. We find Jesus standing to read a portion from the Old Testament prophets. Then he sits to expound it according to the contemporary custom. The term reminds us that there is a lot of ground to cover in communicating the Christian message, that there is a largish body of information and practical skills that must be communicated, that there is intellectual content that must be grasped plus the practical outworking that must follow. The term reminds us that the Christian life has something very definite about it. One cannot exactly 'teach' a fog or a mist; so one does not exactly 'teach' a mystic experience. In New Testament language one teaches a body of coherent revealed truth revolving around Jesus Christ, the *'teaching which accords with godliness'* (1 Timothy 6:3), *'good teaching'* (1 Timothy 4:6).

The teacher spends a lot of time with his Bible. He has some scholarly inclinations – although he must not let them get out of control and become more interested in scholarship than in the church! His ministry is **third** in the life of the church. Apostolic leading and teaching come first. Prophetic teaching comes second, by which I mean not little words of exhortation in the meetings, but mighty and influential revelations of God's truth powerfully applied with words given by the Spirit to the current needs of the hour.

Third comes 'teaching'. Paul emphasises this order in 1 Corinthians 12:28. The evangelist and pastor come in as well but their ministry does not involve such detailed preaching to the church as that of the apostles, prophets and teachers.

The teacher is not a lecturer. His teaching has a lot of content in it but it still has to be **charismatic** teaching. Sheer hard work with the Bible is needed, but mechanical phrase-by-phrase lecturing through the text is not enough. A message from God has to have its own structure and argument for today's needs. It has to have the power of God upon it. Spending time in the presence of God is what makes the teacher truly lively with the liveliness of the Spirit of God. The teacher's word is not purely academic. Although it is high in content, it must still come in the power of the Holy Spirit. His teaching has to be **practical** teaching. It is not simply imparting information as though he were teaching geography or history. His teaching must be **applied** teaching. He is not a 'pure' teacher in the sense of simply being an expositor of a subject. The teacher has to *'labour at the word and in teaching'*, more than others. 1 Timothy 5:17 draws a distinction between the elder who especially labours in this way and the other elders who do not 'especially' give themselves to this aspect of ministry.

I ought to add that these five categories of Ephesians 4:11 are not sharply differentiated. An apostle seems to have a little bit of everything! A pastor can have gifts of teaching as well. Everyone called by God to this kind of Christian ministry has his own particular mixture of Spirit-given abilities. One can even be one thing in one place but another thing in another place. When I travel, God sometimes uses me in giving prophetic guidance to churches and movements of the Spirit. When I am at home in Nairobi I am used quite differently. I know from experience that one can be used one way in one country and in a rather different way in another country. Strange but true! The preacher should not be in too much of a hurry to decide which of the categories he falls in. Let him just be used of God. He can decide later, as he is used by

God, what his mixture of gifts is. In any case others will tell him! He might not always like what they say! Sometimes an evangelist wants to be a pastor, or a teacher wants to be an apostle. The principles are these. Follow the leading of the Spirit, be used in the way God is guiding. Don't be in too much of a hurry. Don't be over-ambitious or under-ambitious. You don't have to push yourself prematurely. God will bring you into your ministry whether it is some kind of preaching ministry or whether it is entirely different. Find the work first. Put the label on afterwards.

Chapter 15

The Ministry of All Christians

We must not think of 'ministry' as belonging only to preachers and notable Christian leaders. Every Christian in the entire church of Jesus Christ has a ministry, and the church of Jesus will not reach maturity until the entire church is playing a part in building the church up in love. The idea that only certain selected individuals in the church are 'ministers' is very misleading. The truth is, every Christian has a ministry and the preachers are to lead the entire church into 'ministry'. The youngest Christian should start doing something for God. This does not mean that everyone does the work of preaching or guiding the church, but there is something for everyone to be involved in. There is a ministry for the youngest Christian and for the oldest Christian. Young Christians may expect their ministry to become larger and more obviously significant.

There are two aspects to the matter which we must consider.

1. **Every Christian has gifts and abilities from God for the service of the church**.

Paul says *'Having gifts that differ let us use them...'* (Romans 12:6). What is a 'gift'? It is **any Christian ability or aspect of Christian character experienced in an unusual degree as a result of the Holy Spirit's working**.

It may be an ability (prophecy, teaching, administration) but it may also be an aspect of Christian character. 'Mercy' is an aspect of one's character, yet Romans 12:8 mentions 'mercy' as a spiritual gift. Some Christians have an unusually tender and gentle way with people. Their character given by the Spirit is their gift. Aspects of one's character may become one's gift.

A gift is something experienced in an unusual measure. Consider the gift of teaching. Every Christian should be able to teach to some extent (Colossians 3:16; Hebrews 5:12) but that does not mean every Christian has the gift of teaching. What makes one's teaching a gift is that one has an unusual anointing from the Holy Spirit enabling the ministry of teaching in an unusual measure. All should exhort (Hebrews 3:13) but not all have the gift of exhortation. All should have faith but not all have the special gift of faith (1 Corinthians 12:28). All should give but not all have the gift of giving (Romans 12:8).

Such gifts come by the anointing of the Holy Spirit. A person may be a 'natural' speaker but this does not become his gift until he is saved and anointed with the Holy Spirit. A person might be generous before his salvation, but he does not have the gift of giving until his giving is unusually full of wisdom because his gift is anointed with the Holy Spirit.

These are what the gifts are. Some are more dramatic than others, but every Christian can know that he has gifts and abilities from God, and that he is to use such gifting for the service of the church.

These are the principles to keep in mind. Every Christian has a gift. No Christian is ungifted. No Christian has all gifts. No one gift is possessed by all Christians. We should become aware of the gifts we have and start seeking to be a blessing to God's people along the lines of the gifts we have. We should not spend time trying to use gifts we do not have. The gifts are for the help of the church. They are not for our own reputation or glory.

The Holy Spirit empowers the gifts. Even though a

90

Christian has some abilities from God he or she does not 'possess' them in the sense of being completely in control. The gifts are the channels along which God often uses us, but on each occasion we shall need the anointing of the Holy Spirit.

2. The second aspect of this matter is that **the preaching ministers are trainers of the entire church of Jesus Christ**. Paul says that when Jesus gave the preachers and leaders to the church, *'he gave them to equip the holy people for the work of ministry, for the building up of the body of Christ, until we all reach the unity of faith and the unity of knowing the Son of God, until we reach to being a fully mature man, until we reach to the measure of the stature of the fullness of Christ'* (Ephesians 4:12–13). The preachers are to equip the entire body of the Christians for the ministry that each and every one of them has.

It is a pity that in some translations of Ephesians 4 it gives the impression that only preachers are in the work of the ministry. Some translations have something like this – *'He gave apostles and others, for the perfecting of the saints, for the work of ministry, for the building of the body of Christ'*.

This gives the impression that the ministry is entirely in the hands of preachers. But there should be no comma after 'saints'. The sense is: *'He gave apostles and others . . . for the perfecting of the saints for the work of ministry'*. The preacher's work of training the saints is *'for the building of the body of Christ'* by means of the whole church being trainers and trainees.

Only as the entire membership of the worldwide church of Jesus is functioning does the church reach maturity. When the entire church is trained in this way it will no longer show childish instability (Ephesians 4:14). *'But rather, speaking the truth in love we are to grow up into him in every way, into him who is the head, Christ. From him the whole body, fitted together and knitted together through every connecting point which gives support, as each individual part is working properly in its own due measure,*

91

causes the growth of the body so that it builds itself up in love' (Ephesians 4:15–16). The teaching ministers are to raise the Christian up to their ministry. This is the point of Ephesians 4:11–16.

Ephesians 4:16 gives a wonderful picture of the universal church functioning as it should. This verse is often applied to the local church. There is not much wrong with that but it must be remembered that Paul was not speaking specifically of the local congregation; he was speaking of the entire church of Jesus Christ on planet earth.

It is a picture of the entire church being consciously dependent on its Lord and Head, Jesus Christ. *'From him the whole body ... causes the growth of the body ... '*. It is from him. The church fulfils its destiny when the church learns to live on Jesus Christ, on his teaching, on his energy, on his guidance, on his spiritual methods. It is a picture of something that will come in the history of the church and which will concern the entire church. It relates to 'the whole body'.

It is a picture of great spiritual unity. The whole body becomes 'fitted together and knitted together'. The unity comes about under the five-fold teaching of those provided by Jesus to his church. Jesus binds together his entire people. The church becomes *'fitted together ... through every connecting point which gives support'*. In a human physical body there are joints and ligaments. There are bones here and bones there. But they are joined together at the joints and they are held together by 'ligaments', pieces of flesh that are tough and strong and hold the parts of the body together.

I am constantly emphasising that this vision concerns the total worldwide church of Jesus Christ. We need to enlarge our vision. The church of Jesus is a gigantic worldwide body. There are many things taking place. There are ministries here and ministries there. It is like a body, a bone here, a tiny bone there, muscles here, organs of the body there. The whole lot is knit together with joints and ligaments. This is what the worldwide church is like. The various preachers of the church in five different groups, are to seek to bind the entire church of Jesus together. Christian unity is already given but it has to be cultivated and enlarged and heightened. The 'connecting points' are to 'give support' to the whole body.

Paul's picture is one of total participation. The whole body becomes *'fitted through every connecting point which gives support'*, and then *'each individual part is working properly in its own due measure'*. It is a vision of every Christian participating in the cause of Jesus Christ. It sees a day when every Christian is 'working properly'. Everyone is in place. No one is attempting things they are not called to do. Everyone is fulfilling the calling that belongs to him or to her. Each part is working 'in its own due measure'.

Paul's picture sees the church growing as it should. The entire body 'causes the growth of the body so that it builds itself up in love'. When the church – led by the teaching ministries – is brought into this total functioning it grows more vigorously than ever. It grows numerically. It grows in maturity. It grows in spiritual energy, and in the beauty of holiness.

Will the church ever become like this? Paul says it will! The story is not ended yet!

This beautiful vision of a totally functioning worldwide church is given to us so that we may go after it. This is always the function of any kind of predictive prophecy. These predictions of the church are given to us so that we may start pursuing the vision immediately.

What is needed? The reality of the five-fold teaching ministries needs to be accepted. We shall not fulfil the vision if we have only teachers and pastors and evangelists. We look to God to give yet more gifted leaders to his church. Then we seek to involve everyone. We give no-one much recognition as 'Christians' unless they are involved in God's church. One cannot be added to Jesus without being added to his people. One cannot have a living relationship with Jesus without there being a living involvement with his people.

When a Christian is living in sin or wickedness, we think that at best he or she is likely to be *'saved through fire'* (1 Corinthians 3:15), assuming they are saved at all. We make that assumption about a Christian living in conspicuous sin, but the same assumption ought to be made about a 'Christian' who is not involved in God's work. Any person who is only a 'sermon-listener' and a lover of the teaching of the church but not involved in the work of the worldwide church is (at best) going to be *'saved through fire'*. Maybe they are not saved at all! A Christian who is not a co-worker with Christ is a very doubtful Christian. Is he or she saved at all?

We must focus our sights on the calling of the church. It is a calling to maturity, a maturity of faith, a maturity of great love. It is important to see that the final goal is love. The whole body *'builds itself up in love'*. This is the nature of the final vision: it is a call to be loving everyone everywhere. If we want to implement God's plan for the church we begin with faith but we aim at love.

PART FOUR

Enjoying the Church

Chapter 16

Enjoying the Energy of the Church

Our theme is 'Enjoying God's worldwide church' and it is
time we began to consider what will be needed if we are
truly to enjoy the church as we should. The worldwide
church of Jesus is to be enjoyed! Joy is a very large part of
the Christian life and it is a very large part of the life of the
church. Any experience of the church which is heavily
burdensome, or legalistic or boring, is lopsided or has
gone off course.

Consider the power and authority of the church. We
generally do not think of 'enjoying' the authority of the
church. The very idea of the 'authority' of the church
makes us think of the pope or of bishops or congresses or
assemblies of clergymen. But the power of the church as
we find it in the book of Acts is a very different thing.
Take a glance at the book of Acts. If you want to know
what the church is meant to be it is the book of Acts
which will tell us. It is a story-book. It is the story of
many of the typical events that happened in the church's
early days. This will tell us what the church is meant to be
like. We shall soon discover that it was vibrant with
power.

1. **The church may expect to enjoy the power of the Holy
Spirit** (see Acts 1:1–4:4). There was a church of a kind in
Acts chapter 1. They were having fellowship with the risen
Lord Jesus Christ (Acts 1:1–11). They were meeting

together and doing some of the business of the church (Acts 1:12–26), and yet the church at this point was without boldness.

Then Acts Chapter 2 tells of a baptism of power coming upon them. It was a sovereign act of God, unexpected and uncontrived. The Holy Spirit was poured out on the whole church.

This power was power for witness. It almost immediately led to their spilling out into the streets. It was power for praise. They started telling the wonderful works of God. It was power for preaching. Peter without preparation preached a message to the crowds which led to three thousand of them becoming converted to Jesus Christ. It was power to produce conviction. The people were cut to the heart (Acts 2:37). This baptism of power led to the miracle of Acts 3:1–11 and the further preaching of Acts 3:12–26. Opposition came from the authorities (Acts 4:1–4) but this did not put an end to the power of the Spirit resting on the church.

2. **The church may look to God for triumphs despite opposition** (Acts 4:5–6:7). After its 'baptism of power' the church faced opposition. Peter and John were summoned before the authorities. Yet they were given great boldness. What strikes us is the great clarity and certainty the apostles had about what they were doing and preaching. They pointed to Jesus as the source of the healing (Acts 4:9–10) and said that there was salvation in no one else (Acts 4:12). A few weeks previously they had not been able to understand the Scriptures, but now they are relating everything to the written Scriptures. They see what is happening in the light of Psalm 118 and Psalm 2. The written Scriptures have become a living book to them under the influence of the Holy Spirit who has been poured out on them.

Soon, because of Ananias and Sapphira, it becomes clear that the church is to be a place of holiness and sincerity. Again the apostles are facing opposition (Acts 6:1–7). Yet the church is going forward with many triumphs despite the opposition of Jews and the hypocrisy of a few members. To enjoy the power of the church is to delight in triumphs in the face of opposition.

3. **The church may expect its influence to spread powerfully** (Acts 6:8–9:31). Stephen, one of God's witnesses is murdered. It looks as if the church is about to be overcome. Yet violent opposition to the church actually helps the church. It actually ensures the spreading of the message even more speedily.

Then the gospel reaches the Samaritans (Acts 8:4–25), the descendants of northern Israel where many gentiles had moved into the area and many Jews had been deported. It was famous as a place of spiritual darkness. Yet there was a further outpouring of the Holy Spirit which made it clear that even the Samaritans could be blessed by God.

Philip was taken to witness to tbe Ethiopian of Acts chapter 8. One is wondering, can this man believe in Jesus? He is from Ethiopia and surely will not want to be converted to Jesus Christ crucified in Jerusalem. But he too is reached with the gospel of Jesus.

Then the power of God saves one of God's great enemies, the persecutor, Saul of Tarsus. He too is added to the church. The church is finding that its influence is spreading powerfully as God's kingdom-power is at work with and in the church of Jesus Christ. We are meant to be enjoying this kind of power in the church.

4. **The church may expect to experience the joys of crossing barriers for God**. In Acts 9:32–12:24, the church overcomes the hatred that was between Jew and gentile. First comes the blessing of God upon Cornelius, who became the first gentile to be baptised with the Spirit.

What hatreds and animosities there were in the ancient world. They were as bad as any racism or nationalism of today. Peter was virtually compelled to speak to Cornelius. The church is led along by the Lord. After Cornelius and his friends were baptised with the Spirit, the church of Jerusalem were prejudiced against what they heard, but Peter explained how God poured out the Spirit on the gentiles as they believed on Jesus.

Then the church went a step further. At first scattered Jewish Christians witnessed only to Jews (Acts 11:19). Then some daring Christians began to witness to gentiles and soon hundreds of gentiles were being saved, and Jewish Christians were having to relate to gentile Christians.

This is all part of the power of the church. Christians have the joy of crossing barriers of nationality and class and language. Christians who have not experienced such joys do not know what they are missing. There are few experiences so enriching.

5. **The church may expect to be led into deeper understanding of grace**. This is what happens in Acts 12:25–16:5. The church of God moved forward faster than ever before. Travelling apostles begin to reach the gentiles in larger numbers, in areas around the Eastern Mediterranean lands. The question was soon raised, 'Could gentiles come into the church without becoming Jews first?' The meeting at Jerusalem discussed this very question. God led them to an answer. 'We believe that we shall be saved through the grace of God in the same way as gentiles are saved by the grace of God'. God is ever leading the church to see new things. These converted gentiles had been such wicked pagans. Did they need to adopt Jewish culture? Did they need to be Jews as well as Christians? No! The lesson was more deeply ingrained into the understanding of the church. Salvation is by grace. The power of God's Holy Spirit leads us into ever deepening appreciation of the truth of God. This is part of the power of God's Spirit. The church may expect to be led into a deeper understanding of grace, through the powerful events that lead us to see that Jesus is salvation. Jesus plus nothing.

6. **The church may expect to challenge the powers of Satan** (see Acts 16:6–19:20). The apostles reached out for God to the worst forms of ancient paganism. We find Paul

in conflict with a demon-possessed girl in Philippi (Acts 16:16–19), then he wins to Jesus a hardened ignorant Roman soldier (Acts 16:19–34), then speaks to intellectual pagan philosophers (Acts 17:16–31). These are extreme challenges. The church is not comfortably sitting in pews learning doctrine. Paul is thrown into prison at midnight but triumphantly sings songs of praise unconcerned about his imprisonment. This is the life of the church! Powerful strongholds of darkness were reached through the power of God. A well-timed earthquake enabled Paul to reach the Philippian jailor. He was not the kind of person who could be reached easily, but an earthquake is a powerful way of opening a person up to consider the things of God! Also, Paul received very striking guidance. A vision led him to cross the sea between Europe and the Roman province of Asia (Acts 16:9). The power of God was with Paul; he pioneers the evangelisation of Europe and reaches such great cities as Corinth (Acts 18:1–28) and Ephesus (Acts 19:1–20). The life of the church may expect to challenge the powers of Satan.

7. **The church may expect its destiny to be fulfilled in surprising ways** (see Acts 19:21–23:11). In Acts 19:21 Paul seems to be settling in a steady ministry in one place. Wonderful things happened in Ephesus and Paul remains there for over two years. Yet God never allows his church to settle down into a routine. After two years Paul knew that he had to press on to Rome. The way would not be as easy and straightforward as one might expect. As he was about to leave Ephesus to go to Rome via Jerusalem, he discovered a plot against him. He was warned of the hardships that were ahead of him (Acts 20:22–24). In Jerusalem, despite his attempts to be as Jewish as he could be (Acts 21:20–26), a riot broke out and he was arrested. Wild accusations were brought against him and he has to stand before the parliament (Acts 22:30–23:10). It all seems a very strange way of getting to Rome, yet Jesus appears to him and tells him, *'you must also testify in Rome'* (Acts 23:11). It is typical of the way God leads his

church. The route God takes seems strange, but God's plans for his church are in hand. Despite all the troubles and trials the church of Jesus will fulfil its calling.

8. **The church may expect to conquer the world for Jesus**. The story of the book of Acts is simply the beginning of the story. Rome seemed, in Paul's day to be the most important place to win for Jesus. The last chapters of Acts (23:12–28:31) tell us of how he got there. Despite immense perils Paul got to Rome! Despite plots against him (Acts 23:19–22), he escapes (Acts 23:23–24). At one point he is almost ambushed and killed (Acts 25:1–3) but again Paul escapes the danger, this time by appealing to Caesar (Acts 25:10–12). Then when he is finally being taken to Caesar even the very wind and waves seem to be against Paul fulfilling his calling. He goes by boat under arrest, and the ship gets stranded out at sea. At one point *'neither sun nor stars appeared ... the storm continued raging'* and the sailors gave up all hope of being kept safe (Acts 27:14–20). But Paul was still kept safe and was at last brought to Rome. Though the gospel was everywhere opposed by the Jews (Acts 28:22) Paul was given liberty to preach and the book ends by telling us that for two years Paul preached without opposition. He had fulfilled his calling to get to Rome. The story of the church will be the same. There is no promise of easy days for the church of Jesus, but there is a promise that the church will fulfil its destiny.

This is the life of the church! It is tough but exciting. The book of Acts is there to tell us what the life of 'the church' is really like. It is far removed from the typical picture that most have of the church of Jesus. But the story of the church is one of joy, of power, of authority. It is full of the anointing of the Holy Spirit. It is a story of triumph, of influence, of fellowship with surprising companions, of the wonderful and amazing grace of God, of resisting and overcoming the devil, of finding fulfilment, of ultimate victory. It is the book of Acts continued to its final end.

Chapter 17

Enjoying the Fellowship of the Church

'Enjoying God's worldwide church' involves rich fellowship with the entire people of God. Fellowship is sharing; it is teamwork in the kingdom of God. It is the joys and friendships that come to us as we put personal ambitions at the service of God and his people.

One aspect of the matter is communication. Throughout the universal church a great deal of communication needs to take place. This is how it was in New Testament times. The church did not keep in touch through denominational structure but it had its own ways of maintaining communication throughout the length and breadth of the church. There was exchange of apostolic letters. There were visits of individuals. There was financial help from one congregation to another. The financial aspect of the fellowship of the international church is an exceedingly difficult matter. Being in a position, as I am, with part of my life linked to the west and the other part deeply involved in third world churches I am in a position to know how much deceit and corruption is involved in religion – even in the Christian, evangelical, circles. I have almost come to the conclusion that wise and genuine financial help is exceedingly rare. Most western churches are so eager to get into 'mission' that they want Third World connections. Most in the Third World who want connections with the west want money, and normally not for the best of reasons! It is a difficult subject. I know from first-hand experience how often generous Christians are bamboozled. Nevertheless – despite all the difficulties – financial help was given from one congregation to another in New Testament times (2 Corinthians 8:11–13). Also there was prayer support between the church and constant sharing of greetings. There was a network of personal contacts that kept 'the churches' obviously and visibly one, yet without their being organisationally or hierarchically united. There are many lessons that we need to draw today from this New Testament description. The New Testament rebukes any kind of isolationism. Many areas of church life are withdrawn, introspective and traditional. Many 'ministers' can only think about themselves and others who might be their supporters. There is need of a wider network, wider contacts in the church of Jesus. We notice the important role preaching ministers had in New Testament times. They travelled around the New Testament church and contributed to the practical unity of the church.

Another aspect to this matter is the need to accept the idea of 'teamwork'. If the church of Jesus Christ is a 'body' characterised by unity and variety then it will mean that the church goes forward by a combination of individualism combined with team work.

Some of us are individualists. We like to do things our own way, have strong ideas of our own, like to have a sense of being in control, and get irritated by the frustrations that come by having to submit in a team! I know; I am one of them! I am glad to say God needs individualists and there is a place in the kingdom of God for them. What would the life of the church have been like if there had not been great individualists like Paul? See him standing alone and refusing to 'cooperate' in Galatians 2:11–14. Read the story of David Livingstone, the pioneer missionary, and see how he had to defy everyone to do what he felt needed to be done to open up Africa to the gospel. To his dying day he scarcely could cooperate with anyone! Think of

Luther, a great individualist if ever there was one. I like the great 'loners' of history.

Yet this chapter is about the 'other side of the coin', the need of fellowship. The more I watch and participate in the church in different parts of the world the more obvious it becomes to me that the church of Jesus goes forward practically by skilful teamwork. The individualists are needed, but fellowship is needed as well. Let me pin-point three aspects of the matter.

1. **The church is enjoyable and powerful when there is a happy fellowship between people and preachers**. Within the pages of the New Testament 'the people' are told *'Obey your leaders and submit to them'* (Hebrews 13:17). Paul was delighted when he could say to his people *'you were all obedient'* (2 Corinthians 7:15), and could say *'we will be ready to punish every act of disobedience'* (2 Corinthians 10:6); *'I will not spare those who sinned'* (2 Corinthians 13:2).

It is obvious that New Testament church life was not a 'one person, one vote' democracy! Leaders were leaders! They were to get to know the will of God one step ahead of everyone else and were to lead the people powerfully and boldly.

Yet the leaders had commands for them, too. They also were under the Word of God. The shepherds of God's flock were told *'Be shepherds ... serving ... willing ... eager ... not lording it over those entrusted to you, but being examples to the flock'* (1 Peter 5:2, 3). They were told to be the kind of people that it would be easy to submit to.

If you want to enjoy the church of Jesus, submit to your leaders! Submit to them in everything that is not sin. You do not need to submit to false teaching or to anything that is wicked. But to everything that is permissible, submit! What if our leaders make a mistake? They often do! But there is no need to panic. When you see a Christian leader making some error or misjudgement in the work of the Lord, just keep praying. If you want to say something, make sure it is tactful and supportive. Make sure the leader knows you are behind him whether he is right or wrong! In earlier days of my own Christian life, before I was in full-time ministry myself, I would support a pastor of a church even if I thought he was wrong! I still do the same today if at all possible.

This is one of the differences between churches in times of spiritual revival and churches in times of decline. Under the influence of western political philosophy we have been corrupted by the idea of 'one man, one vote' democracy. That might be an ideal for political liberty in modern nations but it is a mistaken idea if brought within the church of Jesus Christ. The church is not a democracy and it runs into chaos if it is treated that way.

The church is at its happiest and most powerful when people are energetically involved and yet are happy to follow leadership and where the leaders themselves have a strong sense of destiny and of God's guidance.

The most powerless kinds of churches are those where, whenever there is a forward movement in the life of the church, the congregation has to vote on it at a church meeting. It seems what happens frequently is that the most immature and unspiritual people get up and start picking to pieces the new direction the church is going in. Worst of all are people who are rich or think they are theologically educated. They get power-hungry and want to start ruling the church. The pastor backs down, maybe. Or the church splits. How utterly useless are such church meetings!

No, the secret of enjoying the church is to have a happy spirit of cooperation between leaders and people. The structures of the church should reflect the fact that leaders should lead. Church meetings take place but new ideas are not introduced as 'up for discussion'. In Acts 13 the Holy Spirit gave instructions to a team of leaders (Acts 13:1–3). It was not a case of man-made ideas. Nor was it a matter of rule by church meeting. On the other hand the whole church was kept informed, and when the workers came back they *'gathered the church together and reported all that God had done'* (Acts 14:27).

The preachers are careful not to be too heavy with the people. *'I am not **commanding** you'*, Paul will say on matters where a heavy approach would not be right (2 Corinthians 8:8).

2. **The church is enjoyable and powerful when there is a happy fellowship between the five kinds of preaching ministry**.

Think of the team-work of different kinds of ministry. Ephesians 4:11 lists five preaching ministries. They are not a complete list of every kind of ministry because Romans 12 and 1 Corinthians 12 list others. The ministries of Ephesians 4:11 list deals only with the preaching of the word. Among other things an apostle is a preacher; no pioneering ministry can go forward without the ministry of the Word of God. Yet an apostle has to be so much more than the ordinary preacher. A prophet is also a minister of God's Word. 'Prophecy' is contemporary application of the Word. Even when Scripture is not directly being expounded it still relates to Scripture and agrees with Scripture. The evangelist is a preacher but his task is to take a relatively small area of the message of the gospel and press for response. He is not a teacher. The pastor's task involves shepherding by means of the Word of God. The teacher is the one who covers the greatest area of the Word of God with the greatest kind of thoroughness, But the point is this: **the five kinds of ministry need each other**. In the church every kind of preaching ministry is needed. The church does not grow at any great speed with a pastor who is just a evangelist week by week. After a while the converts get bored with the same kind of preaching and tend to go off to other churches. The teacher is not capable alone of mobilising a church. The various kinds of ministry need each other.

3. **The church is enjoyable and powerful when there is a happy fellowship between all types of people**. In the church there will be rich and poor, academics and non-academics,

male and female. In many parts of the world there will be overseas-workers and local Christians. The church is happiest when these different kinds of Christian realise that they need each other. The church of Jesus does not generally have many rich people, but the church will go forward when the rich Christian seeks to have a spiritual gift of *'contributing'* (Romans 12:8), and yet does not feel that his wealth entitles him to act as managing director of the church. The wealthy Christian may have influence in the world but in the church of Jesus he is 'not to be high-minded' (1 Timothy 6:17) and think he owns the church just because he is wealthy. The average poor Christian around him is likely to have more spiritual power than he has.

The same is true of an 'overseas worker' or 'missionary'. In many parts of the world the average western missionary is a disgrace! Sometimes it happens that the local church prays incessantly, wins people to Jesus all the time, is more spiritually minded than his western counterpart. Then, in the congregation, a 'missionary' arrives. Sometimes that missionary will be less prayerful, less interested in conversions, than the very people he or she has come to help. Matters are made worse if the overseas visiting worker keeps to people of his own nationality. Personally I think that the nineteenth century missionary movement is finished for ever! I did not say that that 'mission' is finished. I said that the nineteenth century European-style missionary movement has finished. People that want to copy nineteenth century missionary methods are as useless and old-fashioned as the pyramids! Their attitudes are normally racist as most third world Christians know – but are normally too polite to say!

The church will flourish when the 'local' and the 'foreign' Christians realise how much they have to give to each other. Churches vary. Some churches in the Third World are dead and decadent. But in many parts of the world there are churches that are lively, powerful, full of worship and praise and prayer. In such churches when a 'foreign worker' arrives he will have to receive much more than he has to give. If he comes as a professional 'missionary' he or she will miss a lot and have little to give!

The same principle is true with regard to academic and non-academic. It is tragic that in the western world, pastors have become increasingly incompetent with God's Word. On the other hand, thorough scholarship concerning the Word of God has become so detached and academic it is of little use to the world of practical ministry. Most pastors have no idea of how to use the scholarly material that is available to help him.

I love great commentaries, and even more I love great expositions, the fatter the better! Alec Motyer's great commentary on Isaiah, F.I. Andersen's massive and brilliant works on the Hebrew text of Amos and Hosea (but requiring a level of Hebrew scholarship beyond most pastors), Don Carson on Matthew's Gospel and John's Gospel, Delitzsch's two volumes on Proverbs, even Luther's eight volumes on Genesis. How I love them and read them, day and night! However there is need of teamwork at this point too. The scholars need the 'ordinary' preachers to get their material to the people, and the preachers need the scholars. What is distressing is that the two sides have drifted far apart. Often when listening to preaching I have been distressed at the sheer ignorance of basic facts about God's Word. Here too is a need for teamwork. The academic seminaries become quite useless if they are not keeping in mind the needs of the preachers and teachers of God's Word in practical situations. Are the scholars to enjoy writing their commentaries in the same way some people like doing crosswords or jigsaw-puzzles? Not many scholars are capable of ministering to ordinary people. This is one of the differences between the past generations of Christians and today. The scholars are not preachers, and the preachers are not scholars.

The secret of enjoying the church and carrying the work of God forward is to look for a spirit of cooperation towards the entire true church of Jesus. *'Do nothing out of rivalry or vain conceit, but in humility consider others better than yourselves. Let each one of you look not only to his own concerns, but also to the concerns of others'* (Philippians 2:3–4).

Chapter 18

Enjoying the Optimism of the Church

To enjoy the church will mean that we enter into its faith and its hope and its love. For the moment let us concentrate on its faith and its expectation.

1. **The church has faith in its message**. 'The church' has limits to it. Not everyone and everything that claims to be 'the church' really is the church. There are indispensable 'marks of the church' in regard to what the church believes. There are some aspects of the church's teaching that are quite indispensable. Within the pages of the New Testament itself we find that there are parts of the gospel that can never be forgotten without destroying the church. There are some religious groups around that call themselves 'church' but they would be better called 'ex-churches' since they have forgotten the gospel. We find stern commands in the New Testament not to depart from the message that has been preached (Galatians 1:6–9), nor to extend hospitality to any who *'goes ahead'* – that is ahead of the apostolic norm – *'and does not abide in the doctrine of Christ'* (2 John 9, 10). The **authority of the first generation of apostles is vital**. *'If anyone thinks he is a prophet . . . he should acknowledge that what I am writing is of the Lord'*, said Paul. *'If anyone does not recognise this, he is not recognised'*, he said elsewhere (1 Corinthians 14:37–38).

Something else that is central are **the main facts of the gospel**. What was at stake when John uttered his stern words in 2 John 10, 11 was the reality of the incarnation. Similar statements are made about the reality of the resurrection and second coming of Jesus. The **reality of sin** is the teaching that lay behind the admonitions of 2 Peter and Jude. No one is truly 'the church' who does not have faith in the reality of God and the reality of **the supernatural**. The nature of salvation by **grace** is a foundation of the church and the church is lost and destroyed wherever this is forgotten. This is the theme of Galatians with its warning in Galatians 1:6–9.

These five areas are clearly treated as non-negotiable by the New Testament writers.

But it is not simply a matter of doctrine. **Experience of Jesus** is equally indispensable. There would have been no book of Acts if there had been no day of Pentecost. There is no church where the people are not clear that they are 'born again' by the Holy Spirit. There is no church where the Holy Spirit is not at work in an obvious and experiential manner.

2. **Enjoying the church demands faith as a lifestyle**. The whole Christian life is a life of faith (2 Corinthians 5:7). The church is the *'household of faith'* (Galatians 6:10). The Christian life begins with faith (Ephesians 2:8) and goes on by faith (Romans 14:1, 2, 23; 2 Peter 1:5; 1 Thessalonians 3:10). By faith we are heir to all of the promises of God (Galatians 3:7–9). The New Testament speaks of 'precious' faith (2 Peter 1:1). Faith is the starting-point of all blessings. Every gift is to be received by faith. All the promises are 'Yes' in Jesus. We have to say the 'Amen' (2 Corinthians 1:20).

To enjoy the church requires we enter into the life of the church and the life of the church is faith! We must continue in believing. Faith goes through testings. There are obstacles and delays and temptations to be faced. It is by faith and patience we inherit the promises (Hebrews 6:12). Saving faith is preserved by Jesus (John 17;

Hebrews 7), but from the human side, **we** must apply our faith, we must continue in faith.

The church looks forward to 'unity in faith'. Its greatest triumphs are to come through faith.

3. **Faith leads on to expectation**. In the New Testament faith and hope and love are intertwined. The Christian life starts with faith; it keeps going because of its hope; it is all leading to love. It is because the Christian is full of faith that he is full of 'hope' in the New Testament sense of the word. 'Hope' in the New Testament means 'expectation', the constant anticipation that God will fulfil all of his promises. Hope is faith looking forward. Jesus said *'Hold on to the faithfulness of God'* (as I believe Mark 11:22 is best translated). *'If you say to this mountain, "Be taken up . . . " . . . and believe that what you say will come to pass, it will be done . . . '* (Mark 11:22–23). Faith has a forward look. It believes that the promises **will** come to pass. Practical, working faith is *'being sure of what we hope for'* (Hebrews 11:1).

The church has a hope for **this** world. True, the church's hope reaches beyond this world, and a 'hope' that is purely earthbound is a worldly thing. Our final hope is the coming of Jesus, the resurrection of the body, the gift of honour and visible glory coming to us from Jesus, and the new heavens and new earth in which is righteousness. If in this life only we have hope in Christ we are of all people the most miserable.

However hope **includes** expectation of God's blessing in this life and then it goes on to see horizons beyond the grave. We have expectations concerning ourselves. We expect to have our needs met (Philippians 4:19), our troubles overcome and the desires of our heart satisfied. Our future and the future of God's church are intertwined. There is more involved than just our personal desires. Our innermost longings are to be fulfilled as and when we are concerned for God's kingdom, God's righteousness and God's church. Solomon was told he could ask for anything but he had just symbolically given himself to God a thousand times over (1 Kings 3:4 precedes 1 Kings 3:5). His greatest longing was to be given what he needed to fulfil his calling in God's holy nation. It will be the same with us. The desires of our heart will be given us as our calling is tied into the welfare of God's kingdom and God's church.

Christian faith is forward-looking and has high expectation for God's church. What are we expecting? Ultimately we are expecting a 'latter-day glory' for the church. We are expecting the church to be built up by the five-fold ministry *'until...'*. Until! There is a future expectation that the church is to fix its eyes upon. Paul holds out the hope of 'the unity of faith'. He has a vision of the church reaching a higher level of faith than was known as he was writing Ephesians. He expected the Christian preachers to continue their work *'until... the unity of knowing the Son of God'*. There would come in the future history of the church a greater and fuller knowledge of the Son of God. Paul was eager to see the preachers of the church leading the entire church into this great day that was to come for the church. He envisaged a day of great maturity, *'being a fully mature man... the measure of the stature of the fullness of Christ'*. It would lead to great stability in the church. The comings and goings of erratic teachers would not be able to disturb the church at such a level of maturity. *'All of this is in order that we might no longer be babies, tossed and carried around by every wind of teaching, through people's craftiness, through trickery for deceitful schemes'*. It would be a maturity which contained a high degree of practical godliness and speedy growth. *'Speaking the truth in love we are to grow up into him in every way, into him who is the head, Christ'*. It would lead to great activities of the church in the cause of Jesus and his kingdom. *'From Him the whole body, fitted together and knitted together through every connecting point which gives support, as each individual part is working properly in its own due measure, causes the growth of the body so that it builds itself up in love'*.

4. **To enjoy the church requires this practical involvement in faith and hope**. We are to believe that great days are coming for the church of Jesus. We are expecting it. We are speaking out our expectation that the gates of hell shall never prevail against Jesus' people. *'I believed and therefore I spoke'* (2 Corinthians 4:13).

Hope makes us ready for conflict. We are in a battle and we expect to win. Our weapons are the weapons of faith and love and expectation. We are ready, prepared for hardships and delays.

Hope makes us sure of victory. We are not expecting to fail. We are sure of final triumph.

Hope gives us courage. It is because we know we shall win we can afford to be bold in the midst of conflict.

Hope is the expectation of seeing God's promises fulfilled. How full the Bible is of promises. We are promised that God will use us, promised that we shall be enabled, promised that we shall be multiplied, promised that we shall be holy. Our hope is our expectation that all of this will be fulfilled. The church of Jesus is the place and location where we are expecting all of the rich promises of God to be fulfilled.

What is your 'hope' in connection with the church of Jesus Christ? I know about the hope of the coming of Jesus (Titus 2:13) and of seeing the glory of God (Romans 5:2) and the hope of resurrection (Acts 23:6) and the hope of final deliverance from sin and all of its consequeces (Titus 1:2). But what about the hope of *'inheriting the promises'* here in this world, promises which are given in connection with God's people?

Every Christian has a calling. Amongst other things 'hope' is the expectation that we shall progress daily in contributing to God's worldwide church. Our greatest happiness will come not simply in thinking about heaven but in aiming to hear Jesus saying 'Well done' to us, in heaven, because of the way we have taken our share in being a blessing in his church. Happiness is connected with serving God and his worldwide people. Happiness will not come to the person who is self-centred and worldly-minded. Happiness is being in the will of God, and the will of God relates to his kingdom and his people. *'Having gifts that differ, let us use them'* in the service of God's people. Let us be full of confident expectation that by faith we shall enjoy a measure of triumphant victory in God's church. There is no life that is happier. 'It is not lost labour to serve God', said John Calvin, 'for he has promised us a plentiful reward, and we shall not be disappointed in our expectation'. God likes to attract us to love and long after success in serving him by the expectation that rich blessings will flow from his generosity. Faith leads on to hope that rich blessings will be poured out upon us as we serve God among his worldwide people.

Chapter 19

Enjoying the Love of the Church

The greatest need in the church is love. There will be no enjoyment of the church unless there is enjoyment of love among God's people. I suppose everyone would agree with that in theory, but somehow we take it for granted. 'Yes, of course', we say, 'love is the greatest need in the church' – and then we proceed to give our attention to something else. Somehow we find ways of not really confronting ourselves with the need to live in the power of the Spirit, which in practice means living a life of dynamic and powerful love towards people.

Over the last half-a-century there has been much talk about church unity. Yet most of the discussion about church unity has been discussion about structures and organisations and reunion movements. Happily, most of that has fallen aside. Most of that discussion was done by people who did not believe in the gospel and, sadly, most of the discussions achieved virtually nothing for the gospel of Jesus. The various reunion movements in old denominations have never had much significance in the real life of the church.

No, real unity is unity in love, visible-love, gospel-love, Jesus-love, love empowered by 'the blood of Christ'. Many want to talk about love but would never talk about 'the blood of Christ'. But, sad to say, those of us who love to talk about the blood of Christ, have often not faced the

116

need to live a life of love in the power of the blood of Jesus Christ. Christian love, Jesus-love, is the greatest and first aspect of the fruit of the Spirit. There is no real joy or peace or long-suffering without love.

It is startling how slow we are to think about love. We somehow imagine that we need to get our doctrine right or our church structures right or the music in the meetings right – but we do not put Christian love very high on our agenda.

But we must face reality, and the presence or absence of love in my life or your life is the greatest test of what we are before God. 1 Corinthians 13:1–3 begins Paul's famous chapter about love by telling us that everything else is useless without it.

The gift of tongues is useless without love. The gifts of prophecy, knowledge and revelation are useless without love. Great deeds of generosity and sacrifice are useless without love.

Paul's description in 1 Corinthians 13:4–7 can be broken down into six ingredients. Love is shown in our attitudes, in six directions.

1. **Consider our attitude towards ill-treatment. Love is patient...** We may be ill-treated or experience unfaithfulness or a brother or sister may deal with us unjustly. **Love is kind**. We are to positively be helpful even to those who we feel have caused us bad experiences in life.

2. **Consider our attitude towards those who are 'above' us. Love is not jealous**. When someone is above us in success, in giftedness, in seniority, we tend to be jealous. It is a sin that affects brothers and sisters and closest friends.

3. **Consider our attitude towards those who are in some way 'below' us. Love does not boast**. When someone is somewhat 'below' us in privileges or attainments or status, we tend to brag or boast or act superior or display our importance! **Love is not proud**. This refers to the way we think about ourselves, the way we reveal how important we think we are. **Love is not rude**. It is not abrupt. It

117

does not brush people aside. It does not put people down. It does not make them feel bad.

4. **Consider our attitude towards self. Love is not self-seeking**. Sin is basically selfishness, self-centredness. Godliness is mainly a matter of breaking free from self-centredness and becoming people of love. It is not wrong altogether to love ourselves. We should have a high opinion of what God can do for us. But this self-love of ours goes too far. We need to love others as we love ourselves (Matthew 19:19).

5. **Consider our attitude towards what we dislike in others. Love is not easily angered**. When we are not walking in love we find within ourselves a spirit of resentment or retaliation. **Love keeps no record of wrongs**. This is the way God treats us. He forgets our sins. *'Their sins and their iniquities will I remember no more'*. **Love takes no delight in evil**. Love will never be pleased when an enemy falls, whether he is exposed, whether he or she falls into sudden calamity. Love is never glad when there is a fall or a failure in the other person. **Love rejoices with the truth**. Love rejoices in every kind of truth. It loves the gospel. It loves mercy and compassion. It loves forgiveness and encouragement. 'The truth' is everything that Jesus wants to bring into the lives of men and women.

6. **Consider our attitude towards any kind of adversity. Love always endures**. It keeps going no matter how painful the circumstances may be. **Love always trusts**. It is the opposite of a sceptical spirit. **Love always hopes**. Even if the situation is terrible, love expects that God will intervene and work in the other person in one way or another. **Love always perseveres**. It does not give up on people easily. For love of people and love of God it presses on without cynicism, without bitterness, without hatred, treating people the way Jesus would if he were present in the body.

The secret of enjoying the church is to make sure that we are contributing to ensure that the church of Jesus Christ is a church that radiates love. Of course we all want others to be loving and tender towards us, but our responsibility comes before our privilege. If we focus on our responsibility to be men and women of love, we shall find others showing us love.

In the life of the church we need to show love – **when a ministry seems to be lost**. Maybe you are a teacher in a Sunday School. One day there is a shuffling around of arrangements and after the changes you are Sunday School teacher no longer! You feel robbed of your ministry! What do you do? If you feel sinned against, obey Matthew 18:15. Then show great love and trust in God.

Or perhaps there are changes in the musical leadership. The organ is replaced by guitars! But the organist has been there for twenty years. He feels that God has given him this ministry of leading the congregation by his fine musical talent. Again it is a time to see how great is one's love for God and for people. Does the organist really care about the needs of the congregation or is he or she just enjoying the organ-playing in itself? Is God reaching a younger group of people and the organ no longer seems as appropriate as it did? It is the kind of situation where a church's love is under test. Will the church mix its musical styles so as to give scope for those with more conservative tastes in music? Might the changes be made more slowly to give the people time to accommodate themselves to what God is doing? It is a time for love to be shown on all sides, love towards God and his kingdom, love towards people and their needs.

We need to show love – **when there are new developments in the life of the church**. Churches do not stand still but many Christians would rather like them to stand still. I recall a time in a church of which I was pastor when the leaders wanted to have two worship services on Sunday mornings rather than one in the morning and one in the evening. It was in South Africa when I was wanting to build a multiracial church, and was having some success in doing so. But one culture in the church tended never to go out in the evenings – partly because it was dangerous to do so. Another culture within the congregation was used to Sunday worship twice, morning and evening. After a while it was obvious what needed to be done. We needed to put both our Sunday services in the morning. The Sunday evening worship appealed to only one section of the church; the morning-time was usable by everyone. We began to have four hours ministry on Sunday mornings but no official meetings for the rest of the day. But what an explosion took place when the leaders first announced they wanted to abandon the Sunday evening service! An article appeared in a denominational newspaper accusing us of wanting a lazy Sunday (did their Sunday mornings involve four hours ministry?)

What breaches of love take place when the work of a church evolves into something bigger and greater and a few traditions get broken. This is a time when love is called for. When there are changes in the congregational life, even the most lively and spiritual churches tend to become gossipy and critical.

We need to show love – **when one feels that there is error or insincerity or self-centredness in a member of the congregation**. Sometimes a brother or sister in the church takes a direction in his life that you do not approve of. It may be that the church focuses more on miracles than ever before. Or it takes an approach towards 'faith' that does not seem quite right. Or it seems to be getting obsessed with 'teaching' to the exclusion of everything else. When the Spirit of God is at work in a church, new things will be happening, but also the church is vulnerable to making mistakes and some of the new developments may not be right, and in a few years – or even a few weeks – will be seen as mistaken trends. Some of the brothers or sisters involved may seem to be in error or perhaps they seem to have devious motives for doing what they are doing.

What does one do? I have no rules. The Spirit of God will lead you. Perhaps you will have to go and speak to one or more of the leaders of the church, or the apostolic leader of the work if there is one – or whatever. Perhaps you will be led by the Lord to do nothing except give yourself to prayer and fasting until things come right. Perhaps you yourself are mistaken and God really is doing something new in the church but you have not yet been ready to accept that what is happening is from God.

But I am making only one point. This is a time for love! Love in those who are right as well as those who are wrong! I have discovered over the years of my being a pastor that in every church dispute one is as much in danger from one's **friends** as one is from one's critics. Sometimes a situation develops in a church where spiritual people want to move on with the Lord but others are less spiritual and are wanting to hold back. We need not decide which group is the spiritual one! Often in such a time those who seem to be the 'spiritual ones' do indeed want to move on with what God is doing, and yet they get very self-righteous. But self-righteousness is just as loathsome to God as sluggishness in responding to God's leading. When a church divides into groups those who are 'spiritual' are in danger of falling into self-righteousness.

Remember 1 Timothy 5:24. Some sins are obvious, others get exposed later. Everything will come out in the end. Remember 1 Corinthians 4:5. Don't judge things too speedily. You can make careful evaluations of what to pray for and what to do, but don't act with a spirit of criticism. Remember 1 Corinthians 13. The church is to be a kingdom of love. You may come to the conclusion that a certain brother or sister in the Lord is not right in his attitude, not right in his opinions or methods. But now you are under test! Will you react with the Holy Spirit of love? Love is the key to everything. Faith without love is nothing. *'Let all that you do be done in love'* (1 Corinthians 16:14).

PART FIVE

The Destiny of the Church

Chapter 20

The Latter-Day Glory of the Church

One reason why the true church of Jesus Christ is so exciting is that the church has a wonderful future. In the first few verses of Isaiah chapter 2 the prophet puts before us his vision of God's 'Zion'. The prophet is using picture-language. It is not that the hill that was in the city of Jerusalem is going to experience some kind of earthquake in which it becomes higher than the Himalayas. No, this is Isaiah's way of putting before us the glorious future of the people of God.

1. Firstly, we note that **the church will enter into unprecedented blessing**. *'In the days to come the mountain of the LORD's house shall be established as the highest of the mountains, and shall be raised above the hills; all the nations shall stream to it'* (Isaiah 2:2). The people of God will experience a day when great blessing will come to God's people. The prophet is using picture-language. Jerusalem was on a hill. God's great plans for the world revolved around Jerusalem. Jesus died there. The Spirit was poured out there. The church began there. One day the church will enter into new and unusual blessing.

2. **The exaltation of the church is a supernatural matter.** *'All the nations shall stream to it'* (Isaiah 2:2). It is a picture of a river of people flowing in great abundance up to Jerusalem. Here is a picture of a stream flowing uphill. Now streams do not normally flow uphill! This is a picture of

something quite supernatural. This is not the result of great human cleverness. It is not man 'bringing in the kingdom' in the sense of bringing about human progress in the story of the church. This is something as supernatural as the day of Pentecost. It does not matter whether or not we can see it coming. It is promised to us and it is quite supernatural.

3. **This exaltation of the church is a voluntary matter**. We read that *'Many peoples shall come and say, "Come, let us go up to the mountain of the LORD, to the house of the God of Jacob; that he may teach us his ways and that we may walk in his paths". For out of Zion shall go forth instruction, and the word of the LORD from Jerusalem'* (Isaiah 2:3).

Here is something beginning with God (for it is supernatural) and yet it results in the people's spontaneously and voluntarily turning to God. It is not after the second coming of Jesus (for there will be no such thing as conversion after the coming of Jesus). It is the people willingly turning to God.

4. **This exaltation of the church is international**. *'Many peoples shall come...'* (Isaiah 2:3). Here is worldwide international blessing. Here is a day when the gospel-command concerning winning nations to Jesus will be obeyed and brought to completion.

5. **This exaltation of the church is practical**. The many people come and say *'"Let us go up ... that he may teach us his ways and that we may walk in his paths". For out of Zion shall go forth instruction, and the word of the LORD from Jerusalem'* (Isaiah 2:3). This spiritual longing is intensely practical. It is a desire to be taught the ways of God, but it is not purely something theoretical. It is a desire *'... that we may walk in his paths'*. These people are actually wanting to walk – to proceed steadily, a step at a time – in obeying God. They are people who want *'instruction'* and *'the word of the LORD'*. Their spiritual hunger is not simply an interest in religion or in theology. They will want to obey God.

6. **This exaltation of the church has social side-effects**. The prophet says *'He shall judge between the nations, and shall arbitrate for many peoples; they shall beat their swords into ploughshares, and their spears into pruning hooks; nation shall not lift up sword against nation, neither shall they learn war any more'* (Isaiah 2:4). This spiritual awakening affects international relationships. It affects the militarism of the world. Justice comes about by God's teaching. War is not taking place, nor is there any preparation for war (*'neither shall they learn war any more'* (Isaiah 2:4)).

7. **This exaltation of the church is lasting**. For apparently a lengthy period it will be true that *'neither shall they learn war any more'* (Isaiah 2:4). It will not be simply a hurried campaign the results of which disappear in a few weeks. Here is something that lasts for decades, perhaps for centuries.

8. **This prophecy lays an obligation upon us**. Isaiah gives his prophecy but then he turns to the nation of his own day (and to us) and says *'O house of Jacob, come, let us walk in the light of the LORD'* (Isaiah 2:5). The reason why such a prophecy is given is that we might *'walk in the light of the LORD'*. Prophecy is not given to us simply to satisfy our curiosity about the future. Rather it is given to us that we might start immediately cooperating with what we know is God's will. Isaiah gives his prediction and immediately says *'Let us walk in the light of this vision the LORD has given to us'*.

This is where we must end our overview of the universal church. I have said little about the 'local' church where all of this has to be worked out. Jesus introduced his entire church (Matthew 16) before there was any talk about 'churches'. He wanted us to see the whole before the parts. Jesus is building his church. It is proceeding whether anyone likes it or not. Jesus has a purpose in this world and it is a purpose that is going to succeed. There is one great advantage of getting a large-scale vision of God's word to us concerning the church before we get down to details concerning life in the local church build-ing, maybe not very far away from us. To see the purpose of God for his whole people will stop us from being small-minded. It will prevent a narrow isolationism. It will perhaps open us up to things that God is doing but which have not yet reached our particular congregation. It will deliver us from narrow denominationalism or turning our own apostolic circle into a sheep-stealing sect. We need to keep our eyes on the glorious future that God has for his people.

A latter-day glory is coming. The writer to Hebrews said *'Encourage one another ... as you see the Day approaching...'* (Hebrews 10:25). What could he see? What was it that made him say *'You can see the Day approaching...'*? Surely it was the success of the gospel. Whoever wrote Hebrews, could see that the gospel was going out all over the Mediterranean area. He knew the world was to be reached and he could see the beginning of it in his own day. For those who have eyes to see it is even more visible in our own day. You can virtually **see** that the day of Jesus' coming is coming closer. No one knows for sure when it will be but one thing is certain, it will not come until this glorious day for the church has come. But it is getting closer and closer. Nation after nation is hear-ing about the gospel. Some so-called 'closed countries' are not so closed as one might think. The day is getting nearer. We are to exercise our faith. We are to stretch forth our hands in expectation. The earth is to be filled with the glory of God as the waters cover the sea. All the ends of the earth will look to Jesus. The kingdom of God must fill the whole earth. Even Israel will turn to Jesus. All nations will be blessed. The uttermost parts of the earth will be given to Jesus as his inheritance. All the ends of the earth shall remember and shall turn to the LORD. Let the nations be glad and sing for joy. In the days of God's king *'the righteous flourish ... He shall have dominion also from sea to sea, and from the river Euphrates unto the ends of the earth ... All kings shall fall down before him. All* *nations shall serve him ... All nations shall call him blessed... '* (Psalm 72).

Here is how we enjoy God's worldwide church. We begin by being sure that we have personally entered into the experience of salvation. We admit our sinfulness. We believe Jesus died for us. We come to him believing that he will receive us. We accept his salvation in faith and give our lives to him. We call upon him to seal us with the conscious experience of his Holy Spirit. We see that 'church' is necessary for our lives and part of God's will for us. Jesus is determined to build his church out of the building bricks of all who know him. His church is his bride, his temple, his body, his holy nation. He builds his church by his five-fold teaching gifts that he gives to the church. He himself is the head but he ministers to his body through apostles, prophets, evangelists, pastors and teachers who train Christians for ministry. We participate in this great plan of God and get to be involved in the worldwide church. We see what we can do to be involved in God's plan to bring worldwide blessing. It will involve our becoming involved in a local church that preaches the gospel, brings men and women into the experience of new birth, and is obviously enjoying the power of the Holy Spirit. But while we enjoy the local church we must not forget it is part of a bigger whole. We encourage one another as we 'see the Day approaching', the day when Jesus comes to bring reward and blessing to all who have been a blessing to his worldwide people.